W9-ABI-814

ADAM SMITH'S DAUGHTERS

To Brinley, who is much missed

Adam Smith's Daughters

Eight Prominent Women Economists from the Eighteenth Century to the Present

Bette Polkinghorn

Professor of Economics, California State University, Sacramento, USA

Dorothy Lampen Thomson

Formerly Professor Emeritus, City University of New York, USA

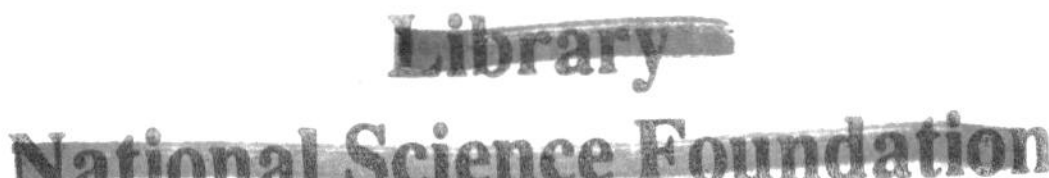

Edward Elgar

Cheltenham, UK • Northampton, MA, USA

Published by
Edward Elgar Publishing Limited
Glensanda House
Montpellier Parade
Cheltenham
Glos GL50 1UA

Edward Elgar Publishing, Inc.
6 Market Street
Northampton
Massachusetts 01060
USA

A catalogue record for this book
is available from the British Library

Library of Congress Cataloguing in Publication Data

Polkinghorn, Bette, 1937–
Adam Smith's daughters: eight prominent women economists from the eighteenth century to the present/Bette Polkinghorn, Dorothy Lampen Thomson.
Rev. ed. of: Adam Smith's daughters/Dorothy Lampen Thomson. 1st ed. 1973.
Includes bibliographical references.
1. Women economists. I. Thomson, Dorothy Lampen. II. Thomson, Dorothy Lampen. Adam Smith's daughters. III. Title.
HB76.P65 1999
330′.092′2
[b]—DC21 98–22239
CIP

ISBN 1 85898 084 4

Printed and bound in Great Britain by Bookcraft (Bath) Ltd.

Contents

Preface

These eight studies are brief intellectual histories of women who have been active in economics. They have been written to remind readers that women have a history in economics, although they have often been overlooked. All came to economics because they hoped to *help* people, to improve the human condition. For the most part, they dreamed of reducing the incidence of poverty. They shared many interests. All addressed what they believed were the important economic questions of their time. All were interested in economic education, whether their targeted audience were beginners in the field or their fellow economists. All of the women found the economic professionals defined the study of economics in an unnecessarily narrow manner which limited its application to issues they thought the profession should address.

In addition, all of the women encountered some career difficulties because they had chosen a field largely occupied by men. Some of them experienced emotional problems as well. In fact, three of the first six contemplated suicide seriously and this is a much higher proportion than is seen in the general population. Yet, they survived and were successful, partially because they were able to overcome the stigma of being 'different' from most women of their time. They chafed in their role as scholars when most women chose more traditional roles. It is hoped that this problem – defining narrowly the appropriate role of women in a society – is rapidly passing. I look forward to an era when diversity is more general and we can offer our daughters – as well as our sons – a climate of toleration and encouragement in whatever career they may choose. I would be very pleased if this book would encourage a person to study economics because the discipline engaged their talent and interest.

In writing this book, I must offer thanks for assistance to a number of people and organizations. Charlene Heinen did a wonderful job of correcting and editing the manuscript and notes. Katie Riley began what I hope is a long and successful writing career by framing the chapter on Beatrice Webb. Three archives offered materials used in my research on Jane Marcet: Archive Pasteur in England and in Switzerland, the Archive of La Fondation Augustin de Candolle, Geneva, and the Archive Guy de Pourtalès, Etoy. I used the library collection of the California State University, Sacramento extensively. Last, I thank Dorothy Thomson for the original idea. She wrote the first edition in the early 1970s. Publishers were not very interested and she finally paid to have it published. Like Harriet Martineau she was convinced that people wanted to know about the history of women writers in economics. She was less lucky than Martineau, and sales were lack-lustre. By the time I came along, nearly 25 years later, I felt the climate had changed and that a revised and expanded edition might be useful and successful.

I added material to each of Thomson's six chapters, including the results of research done on the women since the original publication. I wrote two additional chapters, Irma Adelman and Barbara Bergmann, who are still living and who have contributed substantially to the discipline. Many other women could have been chosen, but this would have resulted in a very large book. I preferred to keep it a small book in the hope that more would read it and be inspired by these women pioneers in our science.

Introduction*

Actually, Adam Smith had no daughters or sons; he was a lifetime bachelor. Yet all economists are in some sense his offspring. We all recognize that scarcity exists and choices have to be made and we recognize that these choices affect the well-being of humankind. Many individuals have written on economics, the science of these choices, in the hope that knowledge of the workings of the economy would lead to a better world for all. Some of these contributors have been women, although their work – particularly in the nineteenth century – was not well known until recently. It is about these contributors that this book is written. From the early writings of the popularizers to the critics of the current residents of the ivory towers, these eight women have distinguished themselves.

The first three, Jane Marcet, Harriet Martineau and Millicent Fawcett, wrote on the subject tentatively when economics was still in the chrysalis stage of development. They were ardent supporters of free enterprise. Their ideology of individualism and the literary forms within which they worked inspired them to purvey simple moral precepts. Economics, in their view, had a close kinship to moral philosophy from which it derived. The kind of philosophy that would give origin to *The Theory of Moral Sentiments* and *The Wealth of Nations* was congenial to them.

The next three, Rosa Luxemburg, Beatrice Webb, and Joan Robinson, were all collectivists in varying degrees. They were drawn to socialism in the belief that 'socialism is, at its root, the effort to find a remedy in social terms for the affront to reason and morality in the status quo'.[1] They wrote on economics with vigour and enthusiasm which testified to their conviction that economics, however scientific, can never be divorced from normative propositions dictated by concern for social welfare.

The last two, Irma Adelman and Barbara Bergmann, are current contributors to economic science. Both concern themselves with income distribution: Adelman with the poorest classes in developing countries and Bergmann with fairness and opportunity in labour markets and concern for children. They criticize our colleagues for defining economics so narrowly that problems in the real world can be ignored. They further criticize that part of the profession that shuns value judgements as they concentrate on developing a 'kit of tools' for the examination and repair of the existing social mechanisms. They are joined, of course, by some well-known male economists who share their views.

The women whose work is seen in these pages would affirm strongly the need both for moral responsibility and social relevance. John Kenneth Galbraith wrote in *The Affluent Society*, 'Once students were attracted [to economics] by the seeming urgency of economic problems and by a sense of their mission to solve them. Now the best come to economics for the opportunity it provides to exercise arcane mathematical skills'. To this Galbraith added: 'Much more than decisions on economic policy are involved. A system of morality is at stake. . . . The central or classical tradition of economics was more than an analysis of economic behavior and a set of rules for economic polity. It also had a moral code'.[2] Kenneth Boulding, in his 1968 presidential address to the American Economic Association, stated: ' . . . no science of any kind can be divorced from ethical considerations . . .'.[3] Robert Heilbroner wrote, 'conventional economics has ensured its technical virtuosity and its internal consistency, but at the cost of its social relevance'.[4]

The women in this book did not confine themselves to a narrowly defined economics. Instead, each viewed her subject in a larger context and identified with problems of current significance. Four of the eight (Millicent Fawcett, Rosa Luxemburg, Beatrice Webb, Barbara Bergmann) engaged actively in politics. Jane Marcet became a prolific writer of educational materials on a great variety of subjects other than economics; Harriet Martineau became a perceptive and influential journalist; Millicent Fawcett became a leader in the women's rights movement. Rosa Luxemburg, caught up by Marx's tempestuous challenge to classical orthodoxy, spearheaded study of the economics of imperialism. Beatrice Webb devoted her talents to exploring the origin and role of certain social institutions, such as consumer cooperation and trade unions, and to learning the causes of why poverty afflicts so many persons. She viewed the appropriate focus of social inquiry not as a quest for wealth but as a 'war on poverty' – a phrase which appears in her diary in 1912. Early in her career Joan Robinson came to the conclusion that static economic theory was barren. Thus she made important contributions first in microeconomics and then in macroeconomics, urging her fellow economists to seek relevance by increasing their awareness of the real world of continuous change. What Beatrice Webb studied for England, Irma Adelman studied for developing countries. She looked beyond mere increases of GDP to the question of whether the poorest citizens of a country received the benefits of development. She evaluated government programmes to determine if they helped or hindered the poor and recommended how economic growth could be made more humane. Barbara Bergmann analysed what she saw as the most important change in the American economy since the Second World War, the entrance of women into the paid labour force. She analysed how the change affected families and how the change could be utilized to benefit all our children.

The interests of these eight women – education, income distribution, women's rights, poverty and methodology in economics – could scarcely contain a livelier list of modern topics. It is a capsule of current concerns and a call to economists to direct our talents to the well-being of all of the world's people.

Notes

*Introduction by Bette Polkinghorn incorporating some material from Dorothy Lampen Thomson's 1973 edition.

1. Heilbroner, Robert (1970), *Between Capitalism and Socialism*, New York: Vintage Books, p. 117.
2. Galbraith, John Kenneth (1958), *The Affluent Society*, Boston: Houghton Mifflin, pp. 142, 289.
3. Boulding, Kenneth (1969), 'Economics as a Moral Science', *American Economic Review*, LIX, pp. 2, 3.
4. Heilbroner, Robert (1970), p. xiii.

1 Jane Marcet (1769–1858)

Early nineteenth century Britain seems an inauspicious time for a woman to become a scholar and economist. Economics was still neither a scholarly nor a popular study. It had, in fact, only recently gained respectability. In the seventeenth century and much of the eighteenth century, many people believed that the study of trade was beneath the dignity of learning, and the opinion that 'the gentleman does not sully his hands in trade' was one that was slow to be overcome. The prevailing view was that 'no gentleman, and especially no self-respecting scholar, would study the subject if he were not forced to'. Thus the serious search and study for the laws of economics was in its infancy. Indeed, the discipline was scarcely discussed outside a small circle of philosophers. That a woman might take up the study and that she might publish the best-selling text in the science was unthinkable. Later a reviewer of one of this woman's books recalled the atmosphere in which she began her career:

> We can distinctly call to mind a period in the history of society when it would have been scarcely less preposterous for a lady to send forth a treatise on a science so abstruse as political economy, than to have commanded a brigade, or manoeuvred a frigate. In the days of our early boyhood, we remember to have heard it predicated, that a girl, in order to be a meet companion for her lord and master, required no fictitious aid of education; that beauty, and sense enough to preserve her from the danger of falling into the fire, were all the qualifications to fit her for society. . . .[1]

Yet, a woman did accomplish the incredible task of writing nearly 30 books, on a variety of scientific and literary topics. Her name was Jane Marcet, and three of her books were on the subject of political economy. Thereupon, she became the first woman to become identified with the science of economics and the first person to undertake seriously the task of economic education.

Jane Haldimand (Marcet) was born in 1769, the same year as Napoleon. She was the daughter of a Swiss merchant and banker, Anthony Haldimand, who lived in London with his English wife. Jane was educated at home with the best available tutors in a cultured and intellectually stimulating environment. In the Swiss tradition, she was taught the same subjects as her brothers. She studied chemistry, horsemanship, biology, history and Latin, in addition to the more usual lessons in art, music and dancing. She was exposed to the writing of Adam Smith and was a very good student. A close relative recalled her as a child who was energetic, responsible, and eager to please. He wrote the following:

> She was barely eight years old, when one evening she heard her grandmother complain that her watch wasn't working well, and that she would gladly part with it for a guinea. The next day she approached her grandmother and proudly handed her a guinea and a half; she had taken the watch, gone to a local watchmaker and concluded a bargain she thought excellent. The poor little girl expected praise, but instead received a scolding. 'My dear child,' the old lady said a bit dryly, 'you mustn't always take everything literally!' Throughout her long life, whether at eight or eighty, Mme. Marcet found it difficult to comprehend that there are two ways of speaking. She could never admit that people altered the truth in any way, whatever the reason.[2]

At the age of 15, Jane was catapulted into adulthood by the unexpected death of her mother in childbirth. Suddenly she was expected to be her father's hostess in addition to managing a large household and a sizable family. Haldimand entertained lavishly, giving two or three large parties a week, to which he invited well-known residents of and visitors to London. It was on these occasions that Jane received and conversed with a great number of scientific, political and literary figures. Here she encountered a handsome and talented doctor who was to become her husband.

Jane had been engaged to marry a cousin in the Navy, but she broke off the engagement due to her father's disapproval. She found herself at the age of 30 – old for the time – with no marriage plans. For a woman with a less secure financial future than Jane's, it might have been difficult to find acceptable suitors. For her it was not. She stood to inherit a full share of the Haldimand banking empire, making her an extremely rich and eligible spinster. As word spread that her former engagement had been renounced, a large number of men presented themselves. Her father allowed her to choose among them, although this was not always the case in the eighteenth century. She chose Alexander Marcet, a London physician, also of Swiss descent. They had a one-month engagement and were married in December 1799. It was an extremely happy marriage, with four children. Jane and her husband were devoted to each other and had a successful life together until his sudden death at the age of 52.

Alexander Marcet's profession was medicine, but his hobby was chemistry – an interest his wife shared. Alexander urged Jane to continue her study of chemistry with Humphrey Davy, who was then lecturing in London. With the support of her husband and the publisher Longman, she wrote her first book, titled *Conversations on Chemistry.* She detailed her motivation in the preface:

> In venturing to offer to the public, and more particularly to the female sex, an introduction to Chymistry, the author, herself a woman, conceives that some explanation may be required. . . . On attending for the first time, experimental lectures, the author found it impossible to derive any clear or satisfactory information from the rapid demonstrations which are usually, and perhaps, necessarily crowded into popular courses of this kind. But frequent opportunities having afterward occurred of conversing with a friend on the subject of chymistry, and of repeating a variety of experiments, she became better acquainted with the principles of that science. . . .
>
> As however, there are but few women who have access to this mode of instruction; and as the author was not acquainted with any book that could prove a substitute for it, she thought it might be useful for beginners . . . to trace the steps by which she had acquired her little stock of chymical knowledge, and to record in the form of dialogue, those ideas which she had first derived. . . .[3]

It was an unheard of success, going to 16 editions and selling more than 160 000 copies in the United States alone. One of the early London editions was read by a bookseller's apprentice – and later chemist – Michael Faraday, who always acknowledged her as his inspiration and 'first teacher'.

After the success of her first book on chemistry, Jane departed from her husband's intellectual interest and struck out independently – this time on political economy. She knew personally both the demographer T.R. Malthus and the financier David Ricardo. Through her brother William Haldimand, who at 25 was made a director of the Bank of England, she had contact with many other members of the London financial community. As her brother and father continued to make their home with the Marcets after Jane's marriage, she was able to discuss current events with them and frequently did so.

The question of the value of the British currency, later to be known as the Bullion Controversy, was of great interest to Jane, her brother and Ricardo. All three took an active interest in the debates on whether the Bank of England should be required to redeem its notes in gold. After an evening at the Marcet home, Ricardo was inspired to write the first of three letters to the liberal newspaper, the *Morning Chronicle* and these articles launched his career as an economist.

The discussions were echoed later when Marcet published her first book on economics, *Conversations on Political Economy.* Here Mrs B is the teacher and Caroline her pupil.

Caroline: I understand that the Bank of England no longer pays its notes in specie?

Mrs B: That is true; but it is owing to an act of Parliament having been passed purposely to grant this privilige to the Bank of England for a specified time.

Caroline: But since the Bank of England is not obliged to pay its notes in cash, it is at liberty to issue any quantity however great. In short, it seems to have discovered the philosopher's stone, for though it may not have found the means of making gold, it possesses a substitute which answers the purpose equally well. . . . And is there not great danger of a bank issuing an excess of notes, when it is not restricted by the obligation of paying them in specie?

Mrs B: A very considerable risk is certainly incurred by such an exemption. An excess of currency produced by the over-issue of bank-notes must . . . cause a depreciation in the value of money, which would be discovered by a general rise in the prices of commodities. . . .

Caroline: But is it known whether the Bank of England has materially increased its issue of notes, since it has been exonerated from the obligation of paying them in cash?

Mrs B: Of that there is no doubt. . . . The strongest argument in favour of a depreciation of the currency is that guineas no longer pass for the same value as gold bullion, which is the natural standard of value of coined money.[4]

Mrs Marcet immersed herself in the study of political economy, which held the double interest of satisfying her mind and her heart at the same time. On one hand, she believed the laws of the economy could be discovered, just like those of chemistry, and she rejoiced in the progress of a science that she hoped would inaugurate a new era for the poor. She hoped that learning the correct principles of political economy would end economic privation for the labouring classes. Later, a relative wrote, 'Here, at once was a great science to reveal and a great cause to promote. She now put all her mind and soul into accomplishing the project'.[5] In one of her letters she revealed her satisfaction in writing on the new subject: 'I can assure you that the greatest pleasure I derive from success is the hope of doing good by the propagation of useful truths'.[6] In the preface to the book she states modestly:

> Political economy, though so immediately connected with the happiness and improvement of mankind, and the object of so much controversy and speculation among men of knowledge, is not yet become a popular science, and is not generally considered a study essential to early education. This work, therefore, independently of all its defects, will have to contend against the novelty of the pursuit. . . .[7]

Thereupon the author launches an undertaking to explain the science that 'treats especially of the means of promoting social happiness so far as relates to the acquisition, possession and use of the objects which constitute national wealth'.[8] The *Conversations on Political Economy* was an attempt to simplify and expand the ideas of the classical school of economics, founded by Adam Smith. The practical importance of the study of political economy is emphasized in the following words:

> The science of political economy is intimately connected with the daily occurrences of life, and in this respect differs materially from that of chemistry, astronomy, or electricity; the mistakes we may fall into in the latter sciences can have little sensible effect on our conduct, whilst our ignorance of the former may lead us into serious practical errors.[9]

There are 22 dialogues – or conversations – between the teacher, Mrs B, and her pupil Caroline. In 475 pages they explore such topics as the right of private property, capital, wages, population, rent, interest, value, price, money and foreign trade.

The market mechanism, for example, is explained in an easy and familiar way in the following exchange:

> *Caroline*: I do not exactly understand why there should be such a perfect coincidence between the wants of the public and the interest of the capitalist.
>
> *Mrs B*: The public are willing to give the highest price for things of which they stand in greatest need. Let us suppose there is a deficiency of clothing for the people, the competition to obtain a portion of it raises the price of clothing, and increases the profits of the manufacturer of clothes. What will follow? Men who are making smaller profits by the cultivation of land will transfer some of their capital to the more advantageous employment of manufacturing clothes; in consequence of this more clothes will be made, and the deficiency will no longer exist. . . .[10]

In one very important respect, Jane Marcet's analysis was different from that of Adam Smith and of her friends Malthus and Ricardo. The important concept was value; that is, what caused some goods to be valuable and others not. Rejecting the idea that the amount of labour contained in a good was the measure of value, Jane preferred the French economist J.B. Say's emphasis on 'utility'. Through Caroline, she defines the utility of a good as 'the real intrinsic value which induces people to give money for them'.[11] After the book's appearance, Malthus wrote to Marcet chiding her for concurring too much with Say's position.[12]

Marcet's was not the 'dismal science' of Malthus and Ricardo. She was more optimistic about the future of the nation than either of these writers for two reasons: 1) she saw no limit to growth of output, income and wealth, as did Ricardo and 2) she was not convinced, as was Malthus, that the working class would erode all increases in the standard of living by having more children. She believed the interests of individuals and of nations to be in harmony. Through her pupil Caroline, she wrote 'Formerly I imagined that whatever addition was made to the wealth of the rich was so much subtracted from the pittance of the poor, but now I see that it is, on the contrary an addition to the general stock of wealth of the country, by which the poor benefit equally with the rich'.[13]

Throughout the *Conversations*, the importance of universal education recurs. After a discussion of emigration, Jane writes:

> . . . the more we find ourselves unable to provide for an overgrown population, the more desirous we should be to avail ourselves of those means which tend to prevent the evil; – such, for instance, as a general diffusion of knowledge, which would excite greater attention in the lower classes to their future interest.[14]

Caroline asks, 'Surely you would not teach political economy to the laboring classes, Mrs B?' And Mrs B replies 'No; but I would endeavor to give the rising generation such an education as would render them not only moral and religious, but industrious, frugal, and provident'.[15] The topic of Caroline's question was to become one of active controversy during the years that followed, and Mrs Marcet was to reverse her own position on this point.

Other introductory books followed and Marcet published texts on a variety of subjects, including astronomy, botany, minerology and physics. Between publications on new topics, she revised her previous books for new editions.

Her writing career did not keep the couple from raising the family that both wanted. Between 1803 and 1809, Jane gave birth to four children, two boys and two girls. Jane was able to employ nursemaids and governesses but she was, nevertheless, particularly close to her growing children and took great pleasure in their accomplishments. As her family had arranged when she was a girl, the two sexes studied the same subjects with the best tutors available. Later Mrs Marcet would write a number of books for children.

Jane's happy marriage ended in 1822, when her husband died suddenly and unexpectedly. She fell into a severe depression. It was two years before Jane Marcet could return to her usual activities of writing and publishing. She credited her Christian faith with sustaining her after her husband's death. As she neared recovery, she prepared a book on a new topic: religion. The book was titled *Conversations on the Evidences of Christianity* (1826) and concerned the circumstances of the writing of the New Testament. The subject explored was whether the gospels were of divine inspiration and were a proof of the divinity of Jesus Christ. The book contained some analysis of the language in which the various accounts were written and demonstrated that she did a considerable amount of research with religious scholars. Thereafter, Marcet added new subjects to her publications: history, literature and humanities.

Over 15 years passed between the publication of the *Conversations on Political Economy* and of Jane's next book on that subject. These years were devoted to books on new topics and revisions of old ones. In the autumn of 1830, however, a new topic presented itself. There had been many disturbances in the English countryside between farmers and their agricultural labourers. Rick-burning and machine-breaking spread, and farmers who used threshing machines received threats. Some farmers in South Wales were concerned about the riots in England lest the unrest spread to their own labourers. In 1831 many of them banded together to form a society to educate their workers 'of their true economic interest'. Jane's son-in-law approached her to write a group of stories that would illustrate the principles of political economy. Earlier she had been opposed to teaching political economy to the working classes, but she changed her mind. She turned her talent to teaching a completely new audience. It was her passion for a peaceful land that convinced her.

In 1833 she published *John Hopkins's Notions on Political Economy*, a collection of nine original stories on economic themes which were intended 'for the improvement of the laboring classes'. It was a primer on political economy for those with limited literacy. Approximately two of every three working men could read in some fashion in this period, although the proportion who could have read this particular book could have been smaller.[16] The stories explored the economic questions of the day, particularly those thought relevant to a person near the bottom of the economic ladder. The economic topics were not treated as comprehensively in this publication as in the *Conversations*, but the tales were more entertaining. The book centres on John Hopkins, an agricultural worker who supported a large family on very meagre wages. He had a simple, inquiring mind and held many distorted views on political economy, which the stories aimed to correct.

The first story, 'The Rich and the Poor', results from John's complaint to a fairy that 'rich men by their extravagance, deprive us poor men of bread'.[17] He continues, 'In order to gratify *them* with luxuries, *we* are debarred almost the necessaries of life'.[18] The fairy offers to help him and his distressed friends saying, 'Shall I, by a stroke of my wand, destroy all the handsome equipages, fine clothes and dainty dishes which offend you?[19] Hopkins assents and witnesses the resulting change, 'the superb mansion of the landlord shrunk . . . and was reduced to a humble thatched cottage . . . the green-house plants sprouted out cabbages . . . the elegant landau was seen varying in form, and enlarging in dimensions, till it became a waggon; while the smart gig shrunk and thickened into a plough'.[20]

All of this reduced the landlord's expenditures with disastrous employment consequences for John's family and friends. He hastens to the fairy, begging her to reverse his previous request. The luxuries and jobs are restored and John Hopkins concludes that 'the poor were gainers, not losers, by luxuries'.[21] Further:

> The rich and the poor have but one and the same interest – That is very strange! I always thought that they had been as wide apart as east is from the west! But now I am convinced that the comforts of the poor are derived from the riches of the rich![22]

He concludes, 'the interest of the rich and poor might go hand in hand, like a loving man and wife, who though they may fall out now and then, jog along together till death parts them'.[23]

In the second story, 'Wages', John asks the fairy to double all wages. The consequent effect of calamitous inflation on prices and employment proves to John that such an act is 'full of danger and mischief' and that he should 'never more apply to the Fairy'.[24] The third story, the allegory of 'The Three Giants' is the most effective in the collection and survives in children's story collections today. The narrator, an itinerant peddler, is to receive a night's lodging as his reward if he pleases each member of his audience. Accordingly, he seeks to satisfy the wishes of John Hopkins's family, one of whom requests a true story; another a story about giants or fairies; a third, a story with a moral. He tells how a small group of shipwrecked islanders discovered three kind and powerful giants – slow but dependable Aquafluentes (stream of running water), fickle Ventosus (wind), and Vaporoso (steam), the truant who needed to be tamed. The three giants proved to be willing and productive helpers who 'worked without board, food or wages'[25] as they ground corn, sawed lumber, wove cotton into cloth, and accomplished astonishing amounts of work. Lucid explanations of the principles of exchange, capital formation, commerce, and real wealth are subtly woven into the tale.

The author left the realm of fantasy with these three stories. The economic topics developed in the remaining stories are best revealed by the alternative title assigned to each:

Population, etc.; or, The Old World
Emigration; or, A New World
The Poor's Rate; or, The Treacherous Friend
Machinery; or, Cheap Goods and Dear Goods
Foreign Trade; or, The Wedding Gown
The Corn Trade; or, The Price of Bread

The above titles give evidence that Mrs Marcet sought to interest both male and female readers. Although undeniably patronizing, her democratic philosophy and her belief in general education are revealed in the following passages:

> Then observing the landlord smile, 'You may think, perhaps,' added he[John Hopkins], twirling his hat in his hands, 'that I ought to be minding my own concerns, and not troubling my head about what is above my capacity.' . . . 'I am very far from thinking,' said the landlord, 'that is it not your business to reflect and consider what is or what is not good for your country. It is not only the right but the duty of every free-born Englishman to do so to the best of his abilities. This, thank God, is not a land in which we are afraid of the people learning to distinguish between right and wrong, even in matters which concern the welfare of the country'.[26]

After publication, Malthus wrote to Marcet approvingly and revealed that he planned to purchase several copies to give away.[27]

Eighteen years passed between *John Hopkins's Notions on Political Economy* and Marcet's last book on political economy, *Rich and Poor*. Despite this length of time, income distribution remained a major topic. In the preface, the author wrote:

> These Dialogues contain a few of the first principles of Political Economy, and are intended for the use of children, whether rich or poor. No portion of that science is more important to the lower classes, as it teaches them that the Rich are their friends – not their foes; that to love and assist each other in all the concerns of life contributes to the happiness of both classes, and to revere the laws of God, which, whether we study them in natural science or by the help of revelation, are all directed to this end.[28]

The setting in this small, 75-page work is a school in a country village, taught by a popular master, Mr B, who undertakes to teach political economy to a group of six eager boys. They do not know what political economy is, but they like all the subjects that he teaches them.

The topics of labour, profits, capital, wages, machinery, price, trade, money, and banks are treated in 13 lessons. He teaches them the difference between rich and poor in the following manner, 'let us call the *rich* all those who are able to live without manual labour; *manual* labour means labour of the *hands*, but in manual labour is included all bodily labour whatever. Poor, we will call those who are indebted to manual labour for their subsistence'.[29]

The boys are told that profits are to the advantage of all parties. They are needed to compensate for waiting and risk. The boys accept the reasoning grudgingly, as one of them remarks 'That's the way that the rich grow richer and richer, while the poor labourer finds it a hard matter to make all ends meet'.[30] After some instruction, the boys reflect, 'a strange sort of a study, this political economy. . . . It seems to belong to or have to do with everything, and that you think you know it before you are taught it; and then, when you begin to learn it, you find you are all in the wrong, and know nothing about it'.[31]

Perhaps because the book was targeted at children, it seems very much simplified and somewhat self-serving. No social reform is advocated and the author argues the equity of the existing system. The 'trickle-down' theory – a variation of the earlier 'a rising tide lifts all boats' – is repeated over and over, as seen in the following passages:

> Do what you will, unless you can increase the wealth of the country, you can neither employ more workmen, nor raise wages, nor in any way improve the condition of the lower classes; whilst an increase of wealth is sure to prove beneficial to them. . . . How often must I repeat to you, that the wealth of the rich cannot increase without the poor being the better for it? Indeed I can defy you, Tom, to point out any way in which the rich can enjoy their wealth without its first passing through the hands of the poor.[32]

Indeed, the harmony of interest of all classes might be summarized by way of the student who observes that 'rich and poor travel together in the railroad of human life cheek by jowl'.[33] Thus, Marcet expressed her belief that all classes could benefit from the wrenching change known as the industrial revolution. She was almost poetic when she wrote in the tenth edition of *Conversations in Political Economy*, 'National opulence diffuses itself, then, on all ranks of people; and, like the sun, spreads its rays all round, from the palace of the sovereign to the cottage of the peasant'.[34]

By mid-century, living standards had risen significantly compared to the second decade when Marcet had written *Conversations on Political Economy*. That the income distribution is emphasized to the extent seen in *Rich and Poor* indicates that higher real incomes failed to affect the question of distribution, or perhaps Mrs Marcet was out of touch with the real economic concerns of the day. From the perspective of more than a hundred years later, one cannot tell which of these theories might be correct.

Mrs Marcet's contemporaries recognized her contribution as an author and educator. *Conversations on Political Economy* was recommended by Malthus and Ricardo. Ricardo believed enthusiastically in the popularization of political economy and commented, 'The most intricate parts of Political Economy might be made familiar to people's understanding . . . and a subject which appears at first view so difficult is within the grasp of a moderate share of talents'.[35]

Other high-ranking critics also acclaimed her work. Macaulay wrote in 1825 that 'Every girl who has read Mrs Marcet's little dialogues on political economy could teach Montagu or Walpole many lessons in finance'.[36] J.B. Say, the author of *Traité d'Economie Politique*, a popular French text, gave Mrs Marcet the compliment that she was 'the only woman who has written on political economy and shown herself superior even to men'.[37]

A more personal comment came from Sir Samuel Romilly and his wife. Lady Romilly commented to the authoress Maria Edgeworth:

> Haven't you been delighted by Mme. Marcet's book? What an extraordinary work for a woman! Everyone who knows the subject is astonished, and people like me who understand nothing about it, or next to nothing, are delighted by the knowledge they have gained from it. One of our former judges who at 83 reads everything that comes out was impressed and truly regrets that he didn't know everything this book taught him when he was still presiding on the bench. How fortunate it would be for the country if our judges, not to mention our statesmen, knew half of what this work contains. You may say that this is a rather bold statement, but I assure you this is not merely my opinion. . . .[38]

Maria Edgeworth herself described a social occasion at Ricardo's and wrote, 'It has now become high fashion with blue ladies to talk political economy. Meantime fine ladies now require that their daughters' governesses should teach political economy'.[39]

By the end of her life, Jane Marcet had published nearly 30 books on a variety of subjects – an almost unbelievable accomplishment in her age. She had maintained a strong interest in the scientific and intellectual questions in the world around her and she had succeeded in communicating her knowledge to others. She wrote to communicate to all what had previously been known to only a few; she was a most successful popularizer. Her work may be judged in retrospect to have been too optimistic. Yet, she was a pioneer, and perfection rarely comes to the path breakers.

Discoverers are seldom the best teachers. Their disciples often prove more successful missionaries than themselves. Marcet's dialogues and stories introduced political economy to a very large number of readers – many times the number who read the works of Smith, Malthus and Ricardo. She never made any false pretensions about her writings. She never overrated her books, nor did she regard herself as an original scholar. She did not advance the state of knowledge herself, but her presentation and techniques were original. Her skilful interpretation enabled individuals to understand what was believed to be true of political economy at the time. Her method of popularizing bridged the road between the scholarly treatises and the textbooks that were to follow. Her work stimulated subsequent writers, launched economic education, and influenced events both in and beyond her time. In addition, Mrs Marcet's stories became the prototype for the work of two women, notable in economics, who were to follow.

Notes

1. *American Monthly Magazine* (1833), vol. 1, p. 1.
2. La Rive, August de (1859), 'Madame Marcet', *Bibliothèque Universelle de Genève*, March, p. 3.
3. Marcet, Jane [published anonymously] (1806), *Conversations on Chemistry*, 1st American edition, Philadelphia: James Humphreys, preface.
4. Marcet, Jane [published anonymously] (1819), *Conversations on Political Economy, in which the Elements of that Science are Familiarly Explained*, 3rd edition, London: Longman, Hurst, Rees, Orme and Brown.
5. La Rive (1859), p. 12.
6. Jane Marcet to Pierre Prevost, 21 September 1816. Archive of the Fondation Augustin de Candolle, Geneva, Switzerland.
7. Marcet (1819), pp. v–vi.
8. Marcet (1819), p. 25.
9. Marcet (1819), pp. 9–10.
10. Marcet (1819), p. 192.
11. Marcet (1819), p. 295.
12. Malthus, T.R. to Marcet, August 1816. Marcet Collection, Archive Guy de Pourtalès, Etoy, Switzerland.
13. Marcet (1819), p. 295.
14. Marcet (1819), p. 167.
15. Marcet (1819), p. 167.
16. Thompson, E.P. (1963), *The Making of the English Working Class*, London: Victor Gollancz, p. 713.
17. Marcet, Jane [published anonymously] (1833), *John Hopkins's Notions on Political Economy*, London: Longman, Rees, Orme, Brown, Green & Longman, p. 1.
18. Marcet (1833), p. 1.
19. Marcet (1833), pp. 1–2.
20. Marcet (1833), p. 2.
21. Marcet (1833), p. 8.
22. Marcet (1833), p. 10.

23. Marcet (1833), p. 121.
24. Marcet (1833), p. 25.
25. Marcet (1833), p. 39.
26. Marcet (1833), p. 155.
27. Polkinghorn, Bette (1986), 'Letter to Jane Marcet, 1833', *American Economic Review*, **76**(4), 845–7.
28. Marcet, Mrs (1851), *Rich and Poor*, London: Longman, Brown, Green & Longman, preface.
29. Marcet (1851), p. 13.
30. Marcet (1851), p. 19.
31. Marcet (1851), p. 23.
32. Marcet (1851), pp. 46, 49, 57.
33. Marcet (1851), p. 13.
34. Marcet, Jane [published anonymously] (1828), *Conversations on Political Economy*, Boston: Bowles & Dearborn, p. 189.
35. Letter of 6 January 1818. Quoted from T.W. Hutchison (1978), *On Revolutions and Progress in Economic Knowledge*, Cambridge: Cambridge University Press, p. 43.
36. Macaulay, Thomas Babington (1851), *Critical and Historical Essays*, London: Longman, Brown, Green, & Longman, p. 3.
37. *Dictionary of National Biography* (1899) vol. 36, London: Smith, Elder & Co., p. 123.
38. La Rive (1859), p. 13.
39. Letter of 9 March 1822 from Maria Edgeworth to Mrs Ruxton. Quoted from Christina Colvin, (ed.) (1971), *Maria Edgeworth: Letters from England 1813–1844*, Oxford: Clarendon Press, p. 364.

2 Harriet Martineau (1802–76)

Little noticed on a small street in the city of Norwich in England is a bronze plaque commemorating the birthplace of Harriet Martineau, the best known of the nineteenth century popularizers of political economy. There was nothing in her childhood to hint at her future success as an authoress. In fact, her early years were most unhappy. She was an isolated, fearful and angry child. Parental tenderness might have alleviated these feelings, but it was not forthcoming. Her mother thought life a hard and serious business and saw affection as an inappropriate preparation for the trials ahead.

A Unitarian family of some comfort, Harriet's parents valued education. They believed that their children ought to be educated to the best of the family's ability and warned of 'the probability that they might sooner or later have to work for a living – daughters as well as sons'.[1] Martineau was taught at home and attended two schools briefly as a boarding student. Her interest was both in academic subjects and social issues and she was recognized by her family as an authority on the national debt at the age of 14.[2]

Her absences from home were happy times for her, as outsiders were more sympathetic to her oncoming deafness than was her family. The latter treated her with distrust and contempt, half believing that her problems were an act to get attention. They thought her dull, difficult and uncommunicative. She sought some comfort in religion and admitted of 'a constant longing for heaven'.[3] Suicide was a recurring fantasy and she believed that 'God could not be very angry with me for making haste to him when nobody else cared for me, and so many people plagued me'.[4] She wrote, 'One day I went into the kitchen to get the great carving knife, to cut my throat, but the servants were at dinner; and this put it off for that time'.[5]

When Harriet was in her teens, her health improved somewhat as she ceased to drink milk – which disagreed with her – and began to drink tea instead. By then she spoke three languages and could read in four. She knew astronomy, history, physical science and was good at mathematics. Still, her deafness troubled her; after a long period of hearing deterioration, she was profoundly deaf. She was also devoid of the senses of taste and smell. After the extent of her deafness was clear, she carried and used an ear trumpet, beginning with an india-rubber tube with a cup at the end for the speaker to take in hand; later, she used an ordinary stiff and bulky ear trumpet. Her isolation increased due to her inability to hear what was happening around her.

When her brother James left home to continue his studies, Harriet grieved at the loss of this valued companion. In response to his suggestion that she try to write, she began to do so; written communication was much easier than trying to hold a conversation. Her first efforts resulted in two articles in the *Monthly Repository*, a Unitarian periodical. Quite remarkably these two early articles showed the direction her later writings were to take. In the first article, 'Female writers on practical divinity', it was obvious that she hoped to teach by her writing. She alluded to successful female writers on divine and moral subjects and urged the teaching of Christian morality by personal example.

Harriet's second publication, 'On female education' was more substantial. The argument supporting education for women was made on economic grounds and involved basic economic principles. She began by denying that physical differences between the sexes indicated different intellectual capacities. She argued instead that apparent differences in the abilities of the two sexes were due to differences in education. She opposed a separate curriculum for each sex and argued in favour of equal investment in male and female children. It was always her belief that when equal amounts of education were available to all children, women would be rendered equal to men in accomplishing any given task. Further, she argued that equal education could be obtained at little extra cost because girls could easily be exposed to the same tutors as taught their brothers. The cost of not providing an equal education could be high, for women were often exposed to the temptations of 'vice and folly' and education would turn them away from such activities. If women were taught the pleasures of intellectual accomplishments, they would be better companions for their husbands and better teachers for their children. The more knowledgeable the mothers of this generation, the better educated would be the next. Hence Martineau showed at this early point that, while she had no formal training in political economy, she understood the principles of human capital investment, marginal cost, opportunity cost and externalities quite well. Further, she understood that the application of economic reasoning could be a successful tool in examining the social questions of the time.[6]

At about the same time, Harriet's brother James brought home a seminary classmate, John Worthington, for a visit. His friendship with Harriet grew to affection, although her parents discouraged his attention on the grounds of his precarious health and poor family. For Harriet's part, the fond feelings she experienced led to a little volume called *Devotional Exercises*.[7] It was a collection of morning and evening sermons and prayers that she first wrote for herself and then for her friend and future fiancé. A publisher was found for the little book and sales were quite respectable.

For his part, Worthington tried to prove himself worthy of Harriet's affections. He had worked his way through college and had then undertaken Divinity School. His high reputation for character and his ability as a speaker won him a position to which many older men aspired. He became pastor of the Unitarian Church in Manchester, a coveted position. The couple became engaged, although Martineau's parents did not give their support. Shortly thereafter, the strain of Worthington's ministry proved too much for him and he lapsed into insanity. After an illness of mind and body of several months' duration, he died.

While it might be imagined that the fragile Harriet would be shattered by this turn of events, she was soon somewhat relieved. She was able to convince herself that the sickly and suffering patient was not the same sensitive John Worthington she had loved. Later she wrote 'there has never been any doubt in my mind that . . . it was happiest for both of us that the union was prevented by any means. I am, in truth, very thankful for not having married at all'.[8]

Martineau's position on the undesirability of marriage seemed hardened after her fiancé's death. She believed marriage ought to be a partnership based on mutual regard and objected to the mercenary nature of most marital arrangements. The lack of attention to points other than the financial arrangements resulted in ill-matched couples suffering through years of misery. Loveless marriages led men to exploit their wives financially and in extreme cases to domestic violence. While outwardly respectable, these hateful partnerships often fostered a climate that resulted in the growth of prostitution – a further exploitation of women. Martineau decried the double standard and she believed men the major contributors to the failure of these marriages; in an 1837 diary entry, she wrote 'If men and women marry those whom they do not love, they must love those whom they do not marry'.[9] Eventually she went so far as to describe the institution of marriage as little more than 'a legal prostitution'. She claimed later that since her fiancé's death her mind had been free of all love affairs. This, in spite of the fact that her name was linked with that of Erasmus Darwin, the eccentric brother of Charles Darwin. It may be that because of the precarious nature of her health, this was not a love affair but just a platonic friendship. As to her spinster status, she concluded at last, 'Thus, I am not only entirely satisfied with my lot, but think it the very best for me'.[10]

At the same time she was worrying over the illness of her fiancé, there was another unhappy occurrence. Her father died, which meant a worsening of the family's financial position. The senior Martineau was a silk manufacturer and an importer of fine wines.[11] The difficulty began with the speculation of 1825. Martineau had resisted the temptation to participate in the initial mania, but when the accelerated trading of assets ended, his business was affected by the resulting devaluation. More than fifty banks closed in a period of six weeks. He struggled to survive, but sales of fine wines and luxury fabrics nearly ceased. He fell ill, and the deteriorating financial condition of his company forced him to change his will, leaving his wife and daughters with only a bare maintenance. He died soon afterward. His son Henry remained in the business but recovery from the trade cycle never came. The few assets of the firm slipped away in time and the company became bankrupt. Mrs Martineau and her daughters were left totally without support.

What was certainly a catastrophe for the family was less so for Harriet because it reduced the opposition to her becoming a writer. The usual occupations of teacher or governess, which served to provide support for educated women who needed a respectable occupation, were closed to her because she was deaf. Her mother urged needlework for a living, but this promised very scant income, so she took up both needle and pen. For many months she did needlework by day and wrote far into the night. Her needlework provided the bulk of her income initially, but her writing became more and more her means of support and ultimately her independence. It was far from obvious at first that writing could provide a living for her and support her mother, but any money she could earn was welcomed by the family. In retrospect, Martineau wrote that the situation brought her 'a wholly new freedom'.[12]

The decade of the 1820s that had begun so badly for Harriet ended on a better note with a great increase in her writing. She continued to write on religious themes and produced a number of short stories with morally uplifting messages. They resembled Sunday school story books but were generally better written. Two of them dealt with topics in political economy, although the author had never read anything on the subject. In 1827, she wrote a tract of 122 pages on the destruction of machinery by workers, a frequent form of social protest at the time. The tract was titled *The Rioters; or, a Tale of Bad Times.*[13] Later Harriet revealed the source of her idea, writing:

> My Globe newspaper readings suggested to me the subject of Machine-breaking as a good one, – some recent outrages of that sort having taken place; but I had not the remotest idea that I was meditating writing on

> Political Economy, the very name of which was then either unknown to me or conveyed no meaning.[14]

Another story, of 135 pages, was written at the same time; *The Turn-Out, or Patience the Best Policy* dealt with the futility of strikes.[15] These and the other tracts that followed were published anonymously, the publisher paying a pound per story for them and selling the copies for a penny each.

It was in late 1827 that Martineau read Mrs Marcet's *Conversations on Political Economy*. She wrote later:

> I took up the book chiefly to see what Political Economy precisely was; and great was my surprise to find that I had been teaching it unawares, in my stories about Machinery and Wages. It struck me at once that the principles of the whole science might be advantageously conveyed in the same way, – not by being smothered up in a story, but by being exhibited in their natural workings in selected passages of social life.[16]

Harriet recalled later, 'I mentioned my notion when we were sitting at work one bright afternoon at home. Brother James nodded assent: my mother said: "Do it" and we went to tea unconscious what a great thing we had done since dinner'.[17]

It occurred to Harriet that she might make the working of the economy seem as exciting as a novel. Profit and loss might be made as suspenseful as a murder story and the level of wages as riveting as fiction. She prepared to write by studying Smith, Malthus and to a lesser extent Ricardo, whose writing she found difficult. She deplored the dry obscurity of the writings then available on political economy because:

> They give us truths, and leave us to look about us, and go hither and thither in search of illustrations of those truths. . . . We cannot see why the truth and its application should not go together, – why an explanation of the principles which regulate society should not be made more clear and interesting at the same time by pictures of what those principles are actually doing in communities.[18]

There were many reasons why the time seemed propitious for such a work. In Martineau's mind the hard times that society faced were due, at least in part, to unwise and outdated laws such as the Old Poor Law. She believed that she had come to see more clearly than others, and particularly the masses of her fellow countrymen, how much the miseries of the current society could be eased by correct and moral behaviour. Reform was the subject of the day and the privileges of government were to be extended to a new class of people who must exercise them with wisdom. Enlightenment was necessary as it would offer information to all upon the science and art of society. Harriet would educate everyone who read her work. This was consistent with her deepest personal beliefs, and the idea began to press upon her as a duty.

Martineau embraced the philosophy of necessarianism, which taught the need for the utmost exertion on the part of each individual to bring himself or herself into line with the natural laws of the universe. Followers of necessarianism believed that for every result there was a cause, and that knowledge of these causes put the individual's fate in his own hands. The philosophy led to strong support for popular education, as it was considered a moral sin for an individual to remain in ignorance. The necessarian believed that individuals could be so formed by education and by an actively diffused morality that they would follow natural laws leading to a happy, vigorous society. Hence, if people wished to improve their lot and reform society, they had to begin by informing themselves. Thus, Martineau thought that a knowledge of the principles of political economy would result in better government and an elevated society.

In espousing the philosophy of necessarianism, Martineau rejected the moral philosophy of sympathy (empathy) that Adam Smith had developed in his *Theory of Moral Sentiments* but had never fully incorporated in his economic doctrine. She believed strongly, however, in his idea of harmony – the view that all classes have the same interest. She rejected Ricardo's belief that the interests of the capitalists and the landlords are directly opposed. She also rejected the philosophy of utilitarianism as expounded by David Hume, Jeremy Bentham, and James Mill, despite the fact that she quoted with approval the utilitarian dictum: the greatest happiness of the greatest number.

There was no doubt in her mind that she was the person to teach the correct principles of political economy to the people. In fact, her only weapon against ignorance was the pen, because women were voiceless before the law. They could neither represent themselves in Parliament nor elect those who would represent them. While reform of the franchise was then under debate, no one believed that women would soon win the vote.

Martineau chose the narrative form of exposition then new to political economy because she was convinced that it was the best form in which to teach the subject. She explained:

> This method of teaching Political Economy has never yet been tried, except

in the instance of a short story or separate passage here and there. This is the method in which we propose to convey the leading truths of Political Economy, as soundly, as systematically, as clearly and faithfully, as the utmost painstaking and strongest attachment to the subject will enable us to do. . . . We declare frankly that our object is to teach Political Economy, and that we have chosen this method not only because it is new, not only because it is entertaining, but because we think it the most faithful and the most complete.[19]

Later, Martineau wrote to Jane Marcet about how she proceeded with the project:

Your conversations on Political Economy first gave solidarity and form to the floating ideas on the subject which I had gathered from newspapers and to you therefore I feel that much of the success of my present exertions is owing. I read your work again and again with delight during the first year after it was put into my hands; and it confirmed a purpose which I had before conceived of acquainting the common people with certain facts of the social system which they do themselves great mischief by misunderstanding; (indeed I was almost a child at that time); and I thought nothing beyond machinery and wages, on which I had written two little tales actually before I knew that their doctrine appertained to the science of Political Economy. By degrees, my plan grew, – in dimensions and in my own favor – but not in that of others. Not a bookseller could I get to undertake the work; the Diffusion Society rejected it, and had it not been for the enterprise of the young publisher who is now reaping the reward of his foresight, I should, I believe been obliged to give up. The merit of the works, I must think very small, its success depending mainly on one circumstance in my method of preparing my tales. The secret is just this. – Instead of preparing my doctrine and my fiction separately, and tacking them together, I digest my doctrine first, and then allow my characters to grow out of the doctrine, and the events out of the characters. The latter is, I fancy, the plan on which all good fiction proceeds, and in all cases of philosophical [formandering?] – of explification of any kind, – the former process must also be adopted. If I had more space, I might dispense with some of my long conversations: but as I can exemplify only the present, the past and future must be illustrated in the ensuing commentary which I am obliged to introduce into all my stories. The remark of your young friend is exactly that which I wish older readers to make, it being generally admitted that prudence ought to become welfare; the nation should take to heart those of its errors by which virtue is robbed of its reward.

I make no apology for the length of my reply to your note, since I have your own word for the interest you take in my labours.

I shall look eagerly for the work you promise to issue, as indeed I do, in common with a multitude, for all that proceeds from your pen. If the mutual interest of our pursuits should lead to a personal acquaintance during my residence in town this winter, or at any future time, I shall have new cause to rejoice in my present labours.[20]

In fact, Martineau's letter to Jane Marcet understated her difficulty in finding a publisher. She had written to a large number of publishers and each had rejected her plan. She told how 'they wanted to suppress the words Political Economy altogether: but I knew that science could not be smuggled in anonymously'.[21] She persisted courageously, convinced of the importance of her undertaking. In the preface she presented the justification, 'If it concerns rulers that their measures should be wise, if it concerns the wealthy that their property should be secure, the middling classes that their industry should be rewarded, the poor that their hardships should be redressed, it concerns all that Political Economy be understood'.[22]

Martineau thought the reluctance of publishers might be due to her inexperience and provincial origin. The publishers she approached claimed that public attention was turned to the Reform Bill and the Cholera (1831). Still she persisted. She stood by her convictions as to the success of the book, telling prospective publishers, 'the people want this book and they *shall* have it'.[23] Amidst the deepest discouragement, Harriet wrote the preface and thought of 'the multitudes who needed it [the stories] – and especially the poor – to assist them in managing their own welfare'.[24] Ultimately, Charles Fox undertook publication reluctantly, with no guarantee of recompense, because he had been counselled by James Mill that Miss Martineau's plan 'could not possibly succeed'.[25] Due to his own financial vulnerability, Fox imposed harsh terms on Martineau, which she accepted with reluctance. She had to guarantee 500 (later 1000) subscribers; if fewer than 1000 copies were sold in two weeks' time, Fox was permitted to cease publication after the first two stories.

In an amazingly short interval after the appearance of the first story – *Life in the Wilds*, a Robinson Crusoe-type tale – it was evident that the project would be a success. The author, then aged 29, later dated her release from financial worry to the publication on 10 February 1832 of the first story of the *Illustrations of Political Economy*. Her conquest was total; she was financially independent and remarked afterward, 'From that hour, I have never had any anxiety about employment than what to choose, nor any real care about money'.[26] Within ten days of publication, the first edition of 1500 copies was exhausted and her publisher proposed a reissue of 5000 copies after any corrections she might wish to make. She received so great a response to her work that her mail had to be collected from the post office in a wheelbarrow.

Her original plan to have the stories appear quarterly was overruled by Fox, who prevailed upon her to have them appear monthly for a period of two years. She reported:

> The idea was overwhelming at first . . . the whole business was the strongest act of will that I ever committed myself to, and my will was always a pretty strong one. I could never have even started my project, but for my thorough well-considered, steady conviction that the work was wanted, – was even craved by the popular mind.[27]

The stories in *Illustrations of Political Economy* were built loosely around James Mill's classical definition of political economy: production, exchange, distribution, and consumption of wealth. The outline was concealed under intriguing titles and chapter headings, intended to draw the reader into the tales from sheer curiosity. The Victorian story titles were beguiling, with not a hint of political economy:

I. Life in the Wilds
II. The Hill and the Valley
III. Brooke and Brooke Farm
IV. Demarara
V. Ella of Garveloch
VI. Weal and Woe in Garveloch
VII. A Manchester Strike
VIII. Cousin Marshall
IX. Ireland
X. Homes Abroad
XI. For Each and for All
XII. French Wines and Politics
XIII. The Charmed Sea
XIV. Berkeley the Banker – Part I
XV. Berkeley the Banker – Part II
XVI. Messrs Vanderput and Snoek
XVII. The Loom and the Lugger – Part I
XVIII. The Loom and the Lugger – Part II
XIX. Sowers Not Reapers
XX. Cinnamon and Pearls
XXI. A Tale of the Tyne
XXII. Briery Creek
XXIII. The Three Ages
XXIV. The Farrers of Budge-Row
XXV. The Moral of Many Fables

Chapter headings were even more disarming; for example:

'Fasters and Feasters'
'A Mushroom City'
'Loyalty Preventives'
'Being Roman at Rome'
'Death-Chamber Soothings'
'How to Entertain Strangers'

In writing, Martineau made use of all the standard works on political economy then available, some of whose authors she was later to know personally. She also made clever use of other materials to round out the settings of her stories. It was said that the Manchester operatives supposed the author 'to have spent all her life in a cotton-mill'.[28] The stories 'Vanderput and Snoek' and 'Feats on the Fiord' were thought to have been preceded by extended residence in Holland and Norway, yet she had never visited either country.

Without the help of a secretary, Harriet completed the 25 stories in the political economy series, each more than 100 pages – a prodigious feat of self-discipline. In her *Autobiography* Martineau revealed, 'As to the actual writing, – I did it as I write letters, . . . never altering the expression as it came fresh from my brain. On an average I wrote twelve pages a day, – on large letter paper . . . the page containing thirty-three lines'.[29]

Favourite theses of each of the classical economists were reflected in her work. She supported Adam Smith's doctrine of the harmony of interests wholeheartedly. She stressed that overpopulation was the basic cause of all social ills. Ricardo's argument for free trade based on comparative advantage and Ricardo's wages-fund doctrine were employed on several occasions. Her acceptance of Say's Law of Markets was implicit throughout.

Some of the stories challenged vested interests and monopoly privileges of the financial and manufacturing community, and they pointed out social abuses in the existing order. Others attempted to demonstrate to working men the futility of striking and rioting. Here she clearly rejected the then popular Ricardian position that the two classes were in permanent conflict because a rise in wages would inevitably result in a decline in profits. Instead, she supported the pre-Ricardian harmony-of-interest thesis between workers and capitalists, since 'the interests of the two classes of producers, Labourers and Capitalists, are . . . the same; the prosperity of both depending on the accumulation of CAPITAL'.[30] Yet, by reason of her treatment of 'a half dozen fundamental topics' on which 'she took a districtly Ricardian stand à la James Mill' she is usually termed 'a disseminator of Ricardian economics'.[31]

Most writers of the period, whether writing for children or for adults, felt obliged to fulfil a serious purpose; Harriet Martineau was no exception. To make certain that her readers had not missed the economic message of the story, she presented at the conclusion a short summary of the economic principles she had treated in the story which 'the reader could either read or as easily ignore'.[32]

The twenty-fifth story in her *Illustrations* served the purpose of being a conclusion for the entire series. It was a text-like discourse of 144 pages titled *The Moral of Many Fables.* Here the principles of political economy, which in 1834 were widely thought to be complete as to definitions, laws, and practical application, were presented. The outline was as follows:

Introduction
Part I. PRODUCTION: Large Farms; Slavery.
Part II. DISTRIBUTION: Rent, Wages, and Profits; Combinations of Workman; Pauperism; Ireland; Emigration.
Part III. EXCHANGE: Currency; Free Trade; Corn Laws and Restrictions on Labour.
Part IV. CONSUMPTION: Taxes
Conclusion

In addition Martineau wrote:

> What, then, is the moral of my fables? That we must mend our ways and be hopeful; or, be hopeful and mend our ways. Each of these comes of the other, and each is pointed out by past experience to be our duty, as it ought to be our pleasure. Enough has been said to prove that we must mend our ways: but I feel as if enough could never be said in the enforcement of hopefulness... [Men] have a vast approach toward being employed according to their capacities, and rewarded according to the works, that is, towards participating in the most perfect conceivable condition of society.... The means and the end [for the good society is] THE EMPLOYMENT OF ALL POWERS AND ALL MATERIALS, THE NATURAL RECOMPENSE OF ALL ACTIONS, AND THE CONSEQUENT ACCOMPLISHMENT OF THE HAPPINESS OF THE GREATEST NUMBER, IF NOT OF ALL.[33]

The stories in *Illustrations of Political Economy* were followed immediately by five more called *Illustrations of Taxation*. Four others, titled *Poor Laws and Paupers, Illustrated* appeared simultaneously. Throughout this period subjects were continually being recommended to Martineau by readers – members of Parliament, cabinet ministers, newspaper editors, factory owners and workers – but some of those subjects, she said, 'had no more to do [with political economy] than geometry or the atomic theory'.[34]

How was the series received? The verdict of the market was overwhelming. Publishers who had rejected the project shortly before made offers, 'the meanest of which' wrote Martineau, 'I should have clutched a few weeks before'.[35] Ultimately 10 000 copies were sold – clearly a best seller, considering the date and the subject. What was the actual readership? Estimates differ. One estimate of monthly sales for the first volume was 10 000 copies, which was estimated to mean approximately 144 000 immediate readers.[36] This might be compared to Mill's *Principles* which sold 3000 copies in four years, and Dickens's novels, most of which had immediate sales of 2000–3000 copies.[37] Using the same ratio between pages and readership as did Martineau's publisher leads to an estimate of 3 000 000 readers at the time of publication, a truly monumental number for that period and likely too large.[38]

Critics of the work differed in their opinions of *Illustrations*. For the most part the periodical press praised the series. The Society for Diffusion of Useful Knowledge bid for the publication rights to the whole series, promising any price after having previously rejected the author's proposal. Readers such as Princess Victoria and Coleridge anticipated the arrival of the next story. Richard Cobden publicly supported the work, and the politician Peel sent a letter of congratulation. The series was published in America and sales were very substantial. Translations were made into Dutch, German and Spanish. Louis Phillipe ordered his educational minister to introduce a French version into the national schools and the Russian Czar did likewise, although both were later to change their minds.

Some economists also viewed Harriet's efforts favourably. Malthus thought she had presented his ideas well. James Mill changed his mind about whether the principles of political economy could be explained in such a form. J.R. McCulloch had doubts about her original proposal but was advised by a correspondent 'that they [the tales] are of extraordinary merit'.[39] To the surprise of many, John Stuart Mill gave the tales a favourable review; he differed with her presentation of the theory on some points but thought political economy had room for both views. In Mill's view Martineau's work did not advance the science of political economy but, judged on its own, merited a favourable reception.[40] (This in spite of a personal dislike for her because of her proclivity for commenting on Mill's unconventional relationship with Harriet Taylor.)[41]

Some reviewers were less charitable. Leslie Stevens, who wrote about Martineau for the *Dictionary of National Biography*, concluded that the tales were an 'unreadable mixture of fiction, founded on rapid cramming, with raw masses of the dismal science'.[42] One biographer judged 'her characters are for the most part wooden, the emotion is synthetic, and the rare attempts at humour are hopeless'.[43] Another wrote:

> We should be loath to bring a blush unnecessarily upon the cheek of any woman; but venture to ask this maiden sage the meaning of the following passage: A parent has a considerable influence over the subsistence-fund of

> his family, and an absolute control over the numbers to be supported by the fund.[44]

Further, she was a '*female Malthusian*. A woman who thinks child-bearing a *crime against society*! An *unmarried woman* who declaims against *marriage*! A *young woman* who deprecates charity and a provision for the *poor*!'[45]

Some modern critics have been less hysterical, but no more charitable. One thought Martineau's work an 'uncritical approach to economic opinion'[46] and an excellent biographer stated that she had a 'knowledge of economics . . . [which was] superficial, impressionistic, and often ill digested'.[47] From the point of view of modern neoclassical theory, the principles illustrated are still valid – opportunity cost, comparative advantage and so forth – but the presentation is stiff and old-fashioned.

Reading Harriet Martineau's fictionalized treatment of political economy today proves disappointing to the modern reader. Too often the author's style reflects her hasty, unrevised composition. By current standards the characters are stereotypes, not persons, and the plots are almost mechanical. In *Weal and Woe in Garveloch*, for example, Angus describes the increase in corn production necessary to keep up with the population:

> as the number of people doubles itself for ever, while the produce of the land does not, the people must increase faster than the produce. If corn produced corn without being wedded to the soil, the rate of increase might be the same with that of the human race. Then two sacks of barley might grow out of one, and two more again out of each of those two – proceeding from one to two, four, eight, sixteen, thirty-two, sixty-four, and so on.[48]

Despite the pretence of the narrative, the stories teach an undigested dogma, and the modern reader may rightfully criticize and regret the author's economic naïvety. Yet even as we deplore the synthetic treatment Martineau gave the subject, we cannot deny that in their day the political economy stories were a successful experiment in adult education. She was not Charles Dickens, or even James Mill, but she became an almost overnight celebrity by writing on political economy. She aimed to overcome the criticisms that political economy was dull and difficult, seeking to present it in a familiar, practical form. Without false modesty, Harriet Martineau acknowledged that she had successfully popularized the subject of political economy, but at no time did she claim originality as an economist. Her own self-appraisal, written in February 1834, appears in the preface to *The Moral of Many Fables*:

> It must be perfectly needless to explain what I owe to preceding writers on the science of which I have treated. Such an acknowledgment could only accompany a pretension of my own to have added something to the science – a pretension which I have never made. By dwelling, as I have been led to do, on their discoveries I have become too much awakened to the glory to dream of sharing the honour. Great men must have their hewers of wood and drawers of water; and scientific discoverers must be followed by those who will popularize their discoveries. When the woodsman finds it necessary to explain that the forest is not of his planting, I may begin to particularize my obligations to Smith and Malthus, and others of their high order.[49]

At a time when labour unions were opposed and workers could be prosecuted for striking, she took a firm stand for the right of labour unions to exist, although their power was to be limited to investigation and to recommending remedies. In 1833, she wrote, 'It is necessary for labourers to husband their strength by union, if it is ever to be balanced against the influence and wealth of capitalists.... The only way is to bring opposition to bear upon the interests of the master, and this can only be done by union.'[50] Her break with the ideology of *laissez-faire* on this subject was supported later by J.R. McCulloch, who regarded prohibitions of workers' combinations as oppressive. Yet, she, as others of her time, supported the fallacious wages fund doctrine which viewed capital primarily as an advance of wages made necessary by the fact that the workers had no property and could not support themselves until the fruits of their labour materialized in a final product. The wages fund doctrine was used to oppose the right of workers to organize, and – as a theory of wages – was not discredited until 1870. It was not replaced until many years later by the marginal productivity theory.

It would be unjust to appraise Harriet Martineau as a person or her entire career solely in terms of her political economy tales, which were written in her early thirties. It was personal economic necessity, a desire to do good and a keen journalistic sense of timing that drew her to write on political economy. She never returned to writing on political economy thereafter. Seen in the perspective of a long life, the political economy tales occupied a very small corner. Indeed, later, writing in her autobiography, she deprecated the work when she wrote, 'After an interval of above twenty years, I have not courage to look at a single number, – convinced that I should be disgusted by bad taste and metaphysics in almost every page'.[51] Doubtless she was also influenced by the belief, then current, that political economy had been fully developed, so nothing remained to be added to its formal structure.

After the political economy stories, there followed a two-year interval between 1834 and 1836 of extended travel in America – a journey that required a voyage of more than 30 days by sailing ship. From this experience Martineau produced two books: *Society in America* and *Retrospect of Western Travel.* Despite lifelong deafness and prolonged intervals of ill health, she was an indefatigable traveller, an astute observer, and a lucid and articulate reporter. Her interests were far-flung and she continued to write on a broad array of subjects: religion, philosophy, travel, sociology and politics.

After a period of invalidism from 1839 until 1844 she built her home, The Knoll, at Ambleside in the Lake District. She remained active, supporting national education and influencing legislation up to the time of her death at age 74.

Determined, dedicated, dogmatic: all of these. Harriet Martineau was a woman of deep conviction who was often unsympathetic to people of differing views. She was not a discoverer but a successful disseminator of ideas. Her stories brought political economy to the public mind, and she tried to teach her readers to use the laws of political economy rather than to oppose them. Although today she is largely ignored by economists, her *Illustrations of Political Economy* was a major accomplishment in early economic education.

Notes

1. Martineau, Harriet (1877), *Autobiography, with Memorials by Maria Weston Chapman*, 3 vols, *Harriet Martineau's Autobiography*, reprinted in Gaby Weiner (ed.) (1983), 2 vols, London: Virago, vol. 1, p. 128. (All subsequent references are to volume 1.)
2. Martineau (1983), p. 71.
3. Martineau (1983), p. 18.
4. Martineau (1983), p. 19.
5. Martineau (1983), p. 19.
6. See M.O'Donnele (n.d.) 'On Female Education: An Example of Early Economic Thinking of Harriet Martineau', Lafayette, Louisiana: unpublished.
7. Martineau, Harriet [published anonymously] (1823), *Devotional Exercises, Consisting of Reflection and Prayers, for the Use of Young Persons, to Which is Added a Treatise on the Lord's Supper.*
8. Martineau (1983), p. 131.
9. Martineau (1877), quoted in Valerie K. Pichanick, (1980), *Harriet Martineau, The Woman and Her Work, 1802–76*, Ann Arbor: The University of Michigan Press.
10. Martineau (1983), p. 133. On page 51 of *Harriet Martineau: A Radical Victorian* (1960), New York: Columbia University Press, R.K. Webb alleges Martineau was at least a latent lesbian because of her close relationship with Maria Chapman. So far as I know, no proof exists.
11. He was a descendant of Huguenot refugees and a producer of two fabrics unknown today: camlet and bombazine. Camlet is a rich, oriental fabric of camel's hair and silk, and bombazine is a fine twill of silk and worsted, often used as mourning cloth.
12. Martineau (1983), p. 142.
13. Martineau, Harriet [published anonymously] (1827), *The Rioters; or, a Tale of Bad Times*, Shropshire, UK: Houlston.
14. Martineau (1983), p. 135.

15. Martineau, Harriett [published anonymously] (1827), *The Turn Out; or Patience the Best Policy*, Shropshire, UK: Houlston.
16. Martineau (1983), p. 138.
17. Martineau (1983), p. 139.
18. Martineau, Harriet (1834), *Illustrations of Political Economy*, 9 vols, London: Charles Fox, Preface, xii.
19. Martineau (1834), Preface, xii–xiii.
20. Letter of 11 October 1832. Marcet Collection, Archive Guy de Pourtalès, Etoy, Switzerland, and Centre de Recherches sur les Lettres Romandes, Université de Lausanne, Switzerland.
21. Martineau (1983), p. 162.
22. Martineau (1983), Preface, xvi.
23. Martineau (1983), p. 170.
24. Martineau (1983), p. 171.
25. Martineau (1983), p. 129.
26. Martineau (1983), p. 178.
27. Martineau (1983), p. 160.
28. Martineau (1983), p. 216.
29. Martineau (1983), p. 195.
30. Martineau (1834), vol. 1, chapter 2, p. 140.
31. Blaug, Mark (1958), *Ricardian Economics, A Historical Study*, New Haven: Yale University Press, p. 131.
32. Martineau (1834), Preface, xv.
33. Martineau (1834), vol.9, Chapter 25, pp. 140–44, *passim*.
34. Martineau (1983), p. 179.
35. Martineau (1983), p. 179.
36. Fletcher, Max (1974), 'Harriet Martineau and Ayn Rand: Economics in the Guise of Fiction', *American Journal of Economics and Sociology*, **33**(4), pp. 369–70.
37. Blaug (1958), p. 129 fn.
38. Polkinghorn, Bette (1995), 'Jane Marcet and Harriet Martineau: Motive, market experience and reception of their works popularizing classical political economy', in Dimand, Dimand and Forget (eds), *Women of Value*, Aldershot: Edward Elgar, p. 77
39. Napier, *Selected Correspondence*, p. 136, quoted in Mark Blaug (1958), p. 130.
40. See *The Examiner*, 1833, *Monthly Repository*, 1834, quoted in Mark Blaug (1958), p. 130.
41. Pichanick (1980), p. 108.
42. Lee, Sidney (ed.) (1893 edn), *Dictionary of National Biography*, London: Smith, Elder & Co., p. 310.
43. Webb (1960), p. 120.
44. *Quarterly Review*, 1833, vol. XLIX, p. 151.
45. *Quarterly Review*, 1833, vol. XLIX, p. 151.
46. Blaug (1958), p. 130.
47. Pichanick (1980), p. 49.
48. Martineau (1834), vol. 2, chapter vi, p. 42.
49. Martineau (1834), vol. 9, chapter xxv, preface, p. vi.
50. Martineau (1834), vol. 3, chapter vii, pp. 49–50.
51. Martineau (1877), 1983, vol.1, p. 258.

3 Millicent Fawcett (1847–1929)

Harriet Martineau's success with her *Illustrations of Political Economy* inspired another woman, who was to continue the line of female popularization of political economy. That woman was Millicent Garrett Fawcett, who was better known for her lifetime advocacy of the right to vote for women. She was a woman perfectly in tune with the proper Victorian world in which she lived.

Millicent Garrett was the seventh child in a closely knit family of ten – six girls and four boys. Her father was a merchant and shipowner in Aldeburgh, in Suffolk, England. He was interested in politics, alert to civic responsibility and active in the affairs of the town. Millicent and her siblings were educated at home with governesses and tutors; both sexes had equal education and privileges and both were taught to think for themselves. She attended a boarding school near London for a time. While many boarding schools taught only needlework, dancing and superficial accomplishments, this one offered scientific subjects and intellectual development. Millicent was reluctant to leave her studies, but her father's temporary business reverses forced her to return home at the age of 16.

Millicent was very fond of her sister Elizabeth, 11 years older than she. After much struggle, Elizabeth succeeded in securing a medical education and becoming the first trained female physician in England. Her success was credited with opening the door to medical education in Britain to women. Henry Fawcett, who became Millicent's husband, had proposed the previous year to Elizabeth, who had refused him on the ground that marriage was incompatible with her career asperations. In addition, he was blind and Elizabeth recognized that 'Mr Fawcett's wife would also have to give up her time even more than most people's need do'.[1]

During the American Civil War, Millicent Fawcett supported the northern cause and developed great admiration for Abraham Lincoln. After his assassination and during a party in London, she expressed the opinion that 'his death was a greater tragedy than would be the death of any European Crowned Head'.[2] Her statement was overheard by another guest, Henry Fawcett, who asked the hostess to introduce him to the speaker. Later, he visited the family in Aldeburgh and continued his acquaintance with this intelligent woman with very liberal views. He proposed marriage in October 1866 (Probably Millicent did not know that he had proposed to her older sister and to a number of other feminists). Millicent accepted his proposal and became engaged to a man 14 years her senior and already a Cambridge professor and a member of parliament for Brighton. He wore his handicap lightly and it was said that his blindness seemed 'scarcely to exist'. In spite of his impediment, he enjoyed fishing, walking, rowing, riding and ice skating. The two were said to be a handsome couple and maintained a very active life in London and Cambridge.

Henry and Millicent were married in April 1867 and took up residence in London and Cambridge. Mrs Fawcett's sister Elizabeth wrote to her mother after having received a report from a visitor to Cambridge: 'She gives a very nice account of Millicent in every way. She thinks she is filling her place at Cambridge most satisfactorily, managing the house well, doing all that Harry wants done & at the same time keeping up her own interest in things independent of him'.[3] Until 1871 Millicent served as her husband's secretary, and naturally, had to read and write for him. They discussed matters of political interest and topics related to his Cambridge lectures, professional writing, and political speeches. She often attended sessions of Parliament, leaving him at the door and climbing the stairs to the 'Ladies' Cage'. It was in the Ladies' Gallery with its heavy brass trellis that Millicent first heard John Stuart Mill speak in favour of the vote for women. He proposed an amendment to the 1867 Reform Bill to omit the word 'man' from the enfranchising clause and substitute the word 'person'. Although the amendment failed, Millicent was much impressed by Mill's argument and the two became close friends. In addition to activities enjoyed with her husband, she pursued her own educational interests, attending two separate courses of lectures.

With her husband's encouragement, Millicent began to write and publish. She sold her first article, 'The education of women of the middle and upper classes' to *Macmillan's Magazine* and received the sum of seven pounds. She donated the money to John Stuart Mill's unsuccessful campaign for re-election, although under the law the money she earned belonged to her husband. There followed other articles on improving education for women and, although she was very young, she built a reputation on the subject. That her prestige was growing rapidly was evidenced by the fact that she was the only woman invited to contribute to the 12 obituary notices of Mill published in 1873, when she was only 26 years old.[4]

The Fawcetts had frequent contact with the publisher Macmillan. While preparing her husband's third edition of *Manual of Political Economy*, Millicent was urged by Macmillan to write an elementary book on political economy for those new to the subject, including children. Her husband agreed and thought her exactly the person to write it. She had a simplifying mind as well as the knowledge needed and a natural distaste for elaboration. The book was in the manner of John Stuart Mill and was extremely successful, going to ten editions in 1911 and selling as many as 30 000 copies.[5] It was translated into at least four languages and used at Harrow and Oxford well into the twentieth century.[6] Macmillan reported that the book was still in print in 1946, an almost unbelievable run of 76 years.

The subject was presented according to the following outline in 200 compact pages.

Introduction
Section I. THE PRODUCTION OF WEALTH
  Chapter I. On Land
  Chapter II. On Labour
  Chapter III. On Capital
Section II. ON THE EXCHANGE OF WEALTH
  Chapter I. Value and Price
  Chapter II. On Money
  Chapter III. The Value of Commodities
  Chapter IV. On the Value of Money
Section III. THE DISTRIBUTION OF WEALTH
  Chapter I. The Rent of Land
  Chapter II. The Wages of Labour
  Chapter III. On the Profits of Capital
  Chapter IV. On Trades' Unions, Strikes and Co-operative Societies
  Chapter V. Co-operation and Co-partnership
Section IV. ON FOREIGN COMMERCE, CREDIT AND TAXATION
  Chapter I. On Foreign Commerce
  Chapter II. Credit and its Influence on Prices
  Chapter III. Taxation

Here is presented the essence of economics as it was understood prior to the appearance of Alfred Marshall's '*Principles*'. Repeated references are made to John Stuart Mill's *Principles of Political Economy*. The emphasis is on microeconomics, but without the benefit of diagrams. Such macroeconomic topics as the benefits of international trade, comparative advantage, and the operation of banks are also included. Acceptance of Say's Law of Markets is implicit in the view that unemployment – a depression in trade – was only a temporary phenomenon and would always be cured by active competition. She described the self-regulating market in the text:

> Where competition is active the effect of a local depression of Trade upon

> wages is only temporary. When wages are below the average and trade is dull, an influence is exerted by these very circumstances to restore wages and profits to their normal condition. Manufacturers will not go on producing commodities at a comparative loss, and intelligent workmen will not go on labouring at an occupation in which they receive lower wages than they could obtain elsewhere. The supply of capital and labour engaged in the depressed trade is accordingly reduced; production is decreased, and the supply being diminished prices rise, and wages are restored to their former level.[7]

While itemizing the 'radical defects' of socialism, not the least of which was removal of 'the prudential restraints' on population growth, Mrs Fawcett conceded:

> The present system does not work so well as to be absolutely incapable of improvement; and though it may not be thought desirable that an alteration of existing economic arrangements should be made in the direction of socialism, we ought to be ready to admit that some improvement is necessary in a community in which five percent of the population are paupers.[8]

She presents an extended discussion on the nature and functions of capital, after which she acknowledges, 'The explanation of the functions of capital has probably presented some difficulty to the beginner'.[9]

She uses a very traditional version of the wages fund, writing that 'Wages depend on the proportion between the wage-fund and the number of the labouring population. If this proportion remains unchanged, the average rate of wages cannot be raised'.[10] She states repeatedly and emphatically, 'A demand for commodities is not a demand for labour. The demand for labour is determined by the amount of capital directly devoted to the remuneration of labour: the demand for commodities simply determines in what direction labour shall be employed'.[11] She saw the need to emphasize her position on the wages-fund with the following statement at the end of the chapter: 'Prove from the propositions enunciated in this chapter that the capitalist is the real benefactor of the wages-receiving classes, and not the spendthrift or the almsgiver'.[12]

The resemblance between Mrs Fawcett's systematic treatment of her subject and that of modern 'outline' books makes the reader feel that some of the latter are lineal descendants of her publication. By means of concise, unqualified statements and homespun illustrations, she sought to promote knowledge of economic principles and their relation to the problems of everyday life. In order to adapt the book for school use, questions were added at the end of each chapter.

In 1874 Mrs Fawcett published four stories entitled *Tales in Political Economy*. She acknowledged her debt of authorship in the preface:

> It is hoped that these little tales may be of some use to those who are trying to teach Political Economy. I cannot let them go to press without a word of apology to Miss Martineau for my plagiarism of the idea, which she made so popular thirty [sic] years ago, of hiding the powder, Political Economy, in the raspberry jam of a story.[13]

The book contains four stories, each with a bright and optimistic tone and is related by 'Captain Adam, an old sailor'.

The first story illustrates the benefits of free trade and the cost incurred by the protection of native industry. The residents of the island, the Srimats, are required by their ruling council to use domestically produced palm oil to light their homes during daytime hours and they are forbidden to have windows or light from any other source. Captain Adam suggests that the islanders could raise their standard of living by using the sun's natural light for their homes and by freeing for other work the two-thirds of the island's population engaged in palm oil production. The islanders perceive this as a threat to their livelihood and chase Captain Adam from their island.

The remaining three stories centre on an isolated Pacific island where Captain Adam and some 20 passengers and crew are shipwrecked. 'The shipwrecked sailors' demonstrates the benefits of division of labour and exchange and the principles of competitive price. The island experiences rising productivity, but the law of diminishing returns is ever present. The principle could scarcely be reduced to more simple terms than the way it is presented in this illustration:

> If you took four boys to a cherry tree, and told them they might have as many cherries as they could gather in twenty minutes, they would get in that time many more than four other boys who were allowed to attack the tree afterwards for the same time and on the same conditions. The first party of boys would gather all the cherries that could be most easily and quickly reached; the second party of boys would have to climb to the topmost branches and strip off every tiny fruit.[14]

The third story, 'Isle pleasant' relates the difficulty of barter and the advantages and disadvantages of using coconuts for money. In the story, the 'Pleasant People', – as they like to be called – learn the difficulties of barter and the advantages and disadvantages of using coconuts for money. There was:

> a great deal of talk about the inconvenience of having no money to make purchases with, and two or three suggestions were made to adopt some natural product of the island as money, and make all exchanges by means of this product.

> The plan was even tried of using cocoa-nuts for money; they were not at all plentiful in the island; to procure them required a considerable amount of exertion, as they grew in distant places, and they were very generally valued for their own sakes, as the milk they contained was very refreshing and the nut itself was wholesome and nutritious. They had, therefore, the two necessary elements of value, i.e., they were useful in themselves, and there was some difficulty in obtaining them . . . But although the cocoa-nuts possessed one quality, 'intrinsic value', which made it possible to use them as money for the purpose of carrying on all exchanges, in two other qualities which should characterize the substance used as money they were found wanting, to a degree that soon led to the abandonment of the idea that they could be used as money. In the first place, although they had considerable intrinsic value, this value varied very much from time to time. Besides the inconvenience arising from their frequent variations in value, the cocoa-nuts were extremely unsuited to be used as money in another respect . . . The bulk of cocoa-nuts in proportion to their value was so great that it formed the strongest possible objection to their use as the medium of exchange . . . but their unsuitability was made evident in another way . . . It was very difficult to use the nuts to make small payments. If a cocoa-nut were divided into twelve equally valuable parts, every one of these, except the shell, would be less valuable a day after it was divided, because the pieces exposed to the air would become first dry and chippy, and then positively bad.[15]

In the fourth story, 'The islanders' experience of foreign trade' the residents learn that exchanging goods for money alone can be useless; it is better to exchange goods for goods. In the story, the trading ship *Carrier Pigeon* set sail with some of the produce of nearly every industry on the island. There are plantains and plantain flour, cloth, plantain wine, articles of clothing and many other items produced for trade. Everyone waits anxiously for the *Carrier Pigeon* to return. At last it is seen and the captain comes on shore. There is no cargo to unload so there is no delay. A sheet of paper, on which is written down the sum realized by the sale of the goods, and a heavy cash-box are brought ashore. The goods brought a good price and the captain remarks 'Gold pieces are as thick as blackberries in San Francisco'.[16] The islanders' pleasure is short-lived, however, when they realize there is nothing left on the island for them to buy with their new riches. They learn that the next time Captain Adam should be instructed to purchase the goods they desire in San Francisco and return with them to the island. Thus were the benefits of free trade demonstrated.

Throughout her life Fawcett was an ardent supporter of free enterprise and free trade. She supported the principles put forward in her books: individual initiative and individual responsibility. She opposed all forms of government intervention and she supported Adam Smith's harmony of interest – that the real interests of all classes were identical.

In 1875 Fawcett published a novel, *Janet Doncaster*,[17] that had as one of its elements the need for a woman to support herself.[18] It contained two themes to which she would return later in her career: first, the sexual exploitation of young women by men, and second, the need to provide an education to women who might have to support themselves. In the novel Fawcett describes the heroine Janet as living in middle-class comfort with her widowed mother. She is persuaded to enter a marriage with a member of the landed gentry whom she does not love. To fulfil a promise to her dying mother, she enters the marriage reluctantly. The reader knows, but Janet does not, that her husband is a hereditary and perpetual drunkard. Soon after the wedding, he drinks himself into a stupor and Janet leaves him. In spite of pressure from those around her, she refuses to return, saying, 'If I went back I should be selling myself, body and soul. I should be no better than those poor creatures in the streets. I should be much worse'.[19] Subsequently, she makes a very small income as a translator. Fawcett hoped that Janet's story would show parents that girls should be given a sound education, lest they have to support themselves some time in the future.

Fawcett also published a group of essays, some of which dealt with economic topics. The first was on the subject of free education and was written originally as a letter to *The Times*. In it, she indicates her opposition to making elementary education free on the ground that doing so would have 'demoralizing tendencies' by removing even more of the natural restraints on population growth than had already been removed by the Poor Law. She writes: 'The poor laws raise the price of provisions and lower the real price of labour . . . by removing the natural restraints on population. . . . It is thus that poverty is perpetuated, and the increased stores of suffering and misery are accumulated which will be borne by future generations.'[20] She quotes John Stuart Mill and Herbert Spencer approvingly and concludes that while compulsory education is necessary to a child's mental welfare, there is no ground for making education free.

Two other essays dealt with the education of women. They contain Mrs Fawcett's reflections on a report of a Schools' Inquiry Commission that had examined the state of middle-class female education and found it deficient. The commissioners had expressed dissatisfaction with the usual curriculum because of the 'want of thoroughness and foundation' and the 'slovenliness and showy superficiality of the teaching of girls.'[21] Too much time, they reported, was spent acquiring 'certain accomplishments of an ornamental, rather than of an intellectual kind, while the cultivation of logical and critical faculties was found to be sadly neglected'.[22] The report credited this condition to the educational deficiencies of school governesses, the indifference of parents, and the lack of vocational opportunities for women. In her essay, Fawcett wrote that parents 'give their sons a good education because it pays; they do not give their daughters a good education because it would not pay'.[23] She continues:

> As long as the height of national prosperity is thought to be attained if the population doubles itself in twenty years; as long as women are considered useful members of society in proportion to the number of their children, so long will their intellectual and moral facilities be neglected. Their education will remain, as it is described by the commissioners, slovenly and superficial, when the highest duties of a wife and mother are practically considered to be to breed children and to keep house.[24]

Henry Fawcett died suddenly in November 1884. After her husband's death Millicent focused her efforts on gaining the right to vote for women, refusing to let other causes distract her from that goal. She was rather like a music box with just one song, and that was suffrage. She believed, as did most of the suffragettes, that once women voted, many of society's problems would disappear; it would be a new world raised to a higher moral plane. She lived to celebrate the victory in England in 1918 and in the United States in 1920.

Honours and recognition came to Millicent Fawcett in her later years. In January 1899 an honorary degree 'in recognition of her work for higher education of women' was awarded by St Andrews University. In 1924 she was made a Dame Grand Cross of the Order of the British Empire and was known thereafter as Dame Millicent. She died in 1929 at the age of 82.

Notes

1. Letter to Newson Garrett, 10 May 1865, quoted in David Rubenstein (1991), *A Different World for Women*, Columbus, Ohio: Ohio State University Press, p. 15.
2. Rubinstein (1991), pp. 10–11.
3. Letter to Louisa Garrett, 26 November 1867, quoted in Rubinstein (1991), p. 18.
4. Rubinstein (1991), p. 32.
5. Polkinghorn, Bette (1993), 'Millicent Fawcett's contribution to economic education: political economy for beginners', unpublished, pp. 8–9.
6. Polkinghorn (1993), p. 7.
7. Fawcett, Millicent Garrett (1870), *Political Economy for Beginners*, London and Cambridge: Macmillan & Co. pp. 106–7.
8. Fawcett (1870), p. 37.
9. Fawcett (1870), p. 33.
10. Fawcett (1870), pp. 98–9.
11. Fawcett (1870), p. 25.
12. Fawcett (1870), p. 34.
13. Fawcett, Millicent (1874), *Tales in Political Economy*, London: Macmillan & Co., preface.

14. Fawcett (1874), p. 49.
15. Fawcett (1874), pp. 54, 55, 57, 58.
16. Fawcett (1874), p. 82.
17. Fawcett, Millicent Garrett (1875), *Janet Doncaster*, London.
18. See Caine, Barbara (1992), *Victorian Feminists*, Oxford: Oxford University Press, p. 206.
19. Fawcett (1875), quoted in Lawrence Goldman, (1989), *The Blind Victorian: Henry Fawcett and British Liberalism*, Cambridge: Cambridge University Press, p. 75.
20. Fawcett, Henry and Millicent Garrett Fawcett (1872), *Essays and Lectures on Social and Political Subjects*, London: Macmillan & Co., pp. 57, 63.
21. Fawcett and Fawcett (1872), p. 186.
22. Fawcett and Fawcett (1872), p. 192.
23. Fawcett and Fawcett (1872), p. 192.
24. Fawcett and Fawcett (1872), pp. 200–201.

4 Rosa Luxemburg (1870–1919)

While the mainstream of traditional orthodox economics continued, as typified by the moderate, well-ordered writings of Jane Marcet, Harriet Martineau and Millicent Fawcett, a counter theme of social, political and economic dissent was building in the ideas of the socialists. Highlighting the excesses of capitalism, this theory reached its highest point in the writings of Karl Marx. Using a model of pure capitalism, Marx predicted that ever larger economic crises would lead to a revolution that presaged the end of capitalism and the birth of a more humane economic system, socialism. For Marx and his followers, the end of this evil and exploitive system was certain; the only question was when and where the revolution would begin.

Rosa Luxemburg was one of Marx's most vocal and able followers, and it fell to her to continue his work and explain why the revolution seemed no closer in the new twentieth century than it had in the nineteenth. Is it possible that socialism would be reached by reform rather than revolt? For Luxemburg the answer was a definite 'no'. Reform of the current system would bring only an altered capitalism, not the democratic and benevolent socialism she so desired.

The youngest of five children, Rosa Luxemburg was born in 1871 into the family of a cultured and relatively prosperous Jewish merchant in the small Polish town of Zamosc, near the Russian border. After Rosa's second birthday, the family moved to Warsaw, which offered improved business opportunities and access to a better education for the children. After their arrival, Rosa fell ill with what was thought to be tuberculosis. She was bedridden intermittently for almost a year and used the time to learn to read and write by the age of five.[1] The initial diagnosis of tuberculosis was wrong; the illness was an inflammation of the hip, which was not treated properly. As a result, the joint was permanently misaligned and Luxemburg walked with a small limp for the rest of her life. She blamed her parents for failing to get a second opinion at the beginning of her illness and believed afterward that the limp made it easier for the police to identify her.

The Luxemburg home was one where education was extremely important and both boys and girls attended the best schools. Rosa won admission to the Second Girls' Gymnasium, a remarkable feat for a Polish Jew. Instruction was in Russian and students were not allowed to even chat in Polish. The Luxemburg family spoke German at home.

Apparently Rosa was also acquainted with Yiddish, although it was never used in the household. Later she could sometimes whisper in Yiddish to fellow prisoners in jail, as none of the guards spoke a word of it.

While her father was in sympathy with the Polish nationalist movement, he was not politically active. This was not the case for his daughter Rosa. Her formal studies acquainted her with the writings of Adam Smith and the other moral philosophers and her natural inclinations led her to the illicit writings of the radical movement. There she read the ideas of Marx and Engels. In her last year at school she was thought to have revolutionary sympathies and was judged 'not amenable to discipline'.[2] She obtained the highest results in all of her final examinations but was denied the medal for her achievements 'on account of her rebellious attitude toward the authorities'.[3]

When Rosa's views and activities became known to the local authorities, she feared she would soon be arrested. She was aware that there were many political exiles in Zurich and that she could continue her education there. Hence, it was arranged that she would slip across the border of Russian Poland to join the colony of radical thinkers in Switzerland. Many had made the trip before and it was not expected to be particularly dangerous. During the journey an amusing incident occurred, verified by Luxemburg herself.[4] She was unable to obtain regular transport for the crossing, so an older friend approached the local Catholic priest and claimed that a Jewish girl wished to be baptized in order to marry her lover but 'owing to the violent opposition of her family, could only do so abroad'.[5] The sympathetic priest arranged for Luxemburg to be transported to Switzerland in a peasant's cart, hidden by a pile of straw. There she began a new life as a student *émigrée* at a time when socialist and revolutionary ideas were in a crucial stage of development.

The students discussed their ideas and theories of socialism endlessly. They debated the meaning of the Marxian model and its possible application to their homelands. What tactics would be most conducive to bring about the final revolution? How should workers be educated to their real interest? What should be the role of the intellectuals? How centralized versus how democratic could the new governments be? For Rosa, these were important and exciting questions. While she was attracted to the study of literature, botany, geology and mathematics, none of these held her lifetime interest as did political economy. To her it was politics and economics that would change the world and this is what she hoped to do. Her studies and her new revolutionary friends were stimulating and their ideas riveting. She was able to think, to discuss and to write her new ideas. At this time another important event occurred: she met the man who was to be the love of her life. Leo Jogiches was a political organizer who had escaped from the town of Wilno in Lithuania after some local labour disturbances. He was 23 and she was 20. From here to the end of Rosa's life, her professional and her personal lives would be intertwined.

In the early years of their relationship, Luxemburg found Jogiches irresistible. Handsome, radical, experienced in organizing conspiracies, and relatively well off, he was her dream. That she should have such a lover was quite beyond her hopes, and his less desirable traits were easy to overlook. In fact, he was also intensely suspicious, evasive, arrogant and jealous – qualities that were to become obvious later.

Even though Leo was only three years older than Rosa, he served first as her teacher and mentor, instructing and guiding her in the practical aspects of being a revolutionary. If he was less able in theorizing and writing about the intellectual framework of socialism, she didn't notice. When they became lovers, he forbade her to reveal this fact. He was secretive in other ways as well, using at least a dozen different names in a student, *émigré* community where it hardly seemed necessary. At the same time he proposed to better known socialists a series of publication schemes that would have enriched himself and left the authors with very little. This rather odd behaviour led some of his colleagues to question his morals and motives. But none of this lessened Rosa's feelings for him or alerted her to the problems she might face with him in the future; she was simply too much in love to notice.

Rosa earned her doctorate in law and philosophy at the University of Zurich in 1897, after having first pursued courses in natural sciences and mathematics. Her doctoral thesis, '*The Industrial Development of Poland*' was her first contribution to economics. It achieved immediate commercial publication and was widely reviewed in Germany, Poland and Russia. In it Luxemburg analysed the growth of Polish industry in the nineteenth century, demonstrating that Russian Poland had become so dependent on the Russian market that political demands for Polish independence were unrealistic. The economic evidence that she assembled to support her conclusion provided the basis for her continuing stand on this question. Her opposition to Polish independence was very unpopular with the old-line Polish nationalist–socialists and served to alienate many individuals who were her natural allies.

Finished with her studies, Rosa moved to Berlin, the centre of the socialist movement. To gain German citizenship and to prevent deportation, she contracted a fraudulent marriage with the son of a friend.[6]

Her heart was still with Leo Jogiches, however, and there is no evidence that she ever lived with this husband of convenience.

Her activities ranged from organizing miners in Silesia[7] to writing a book condemning revisionism, the idea that socialism might be attained by reform of capitalism. Adherents of this view argued for a modification of the Marxian arguments. They believed that capitalism had a far greater potential for survival than Marx had realized and they emphasized the fact that capitalism might be modified to bring redistribution of income and wealth. They advocated reform by means of continuing pressure by trade unions and by cooperatives of producers and consumers. Reform could be accomplished, they believed, by modifying the existing economic system and thus avoiding the armed revolution thought necessary by orthodox Marxists. Luxemburg's detailed critique of this evolutionary path to socialism is still part of orthodox Marxism. In *Social Reform or Revolution* she wrote:

> People who pronounce themselves in favor of the method of legislative reform in place and in contradistinction to the conquest of political power and social revolution do not really choose a more tranquil, calmer and slower road to the same goal, but a different goal. Instead of a stand for the establishment of a new society they take a stand for surface modifications of the old society.... Our program becomes not the realization of socialism, but the reform of capitalism; not the suppression of the system of wage labor, but the diminution of exploitation, that is, the suppression of the abuses of capitalism instead of the suppression of capitalism itself.[8]

Meanwhile, her relationship with Jogiches deteriorated. Claiming to be finishing his own degree, he refused for two years to join her in Berlin. In truth, he feared being eclipsed by her success. For her part, she insisted on maintaining her successful professional life as well as the dream of a more traditional home. She continued to hope for the bourgeois life of wife and mother – just the life Jogiches wished to escape. It was the classic case of a woman of great capabilities choosing a life partner incompatible with her private goals – the *Smart Women, Foolish Choices* of an earlier age. Her letters to Jogiches were alternately demanding and begging, but her personal unhappiness did not keep her from continuing the revolutionary struggle.

Luxemburg became one of the acknowledged leaders of the left wing of the German socialists, participating in every undertaking that she believed would advance the revolution of the proletariat against the bourgeoisie. She was in the centre of doctrinal and tactical disputes, a leader in the affairs of the Polish, Russian and German Socialist parties, an organizer for mass activities, a principal speaker at Socialist meetings and congresses, and a featured writer for theoretical and popular journals. Always working on behalf of international socialism, she battled against Polish nationalism, the adoption of revisionist policies and the hated capitalist system. Her intense political agitation, her vitriolic polemics, her advocacy of mass strikes, and her uncompromising opposition to war made prosecution and jail a continuing threat.

In 1907 the German Social Democratic Party founded a party training school in Berlin, and Rosa Luxemburg was appointed lecturer in political economy. The students were quite diverse, ranging from workers with intellectual promise to party initiates who knew little of theoretical Marxism. It was intended that the students would return to their homes and become teachers and activists there. Luxemburg liked the work very much and began a book, *Introduction to Political Economy* to supplement her lectures.[9] It was during the writing of this elementary Marxist text that she encountered difficulties in Marx's work that she could not resolve. Of this she wrote, 'I could not succeed in depicting the total process of capitalistic production in all its practical relations as well as its historical limitations with sufficient clarity'.[10] Marx did not prove to her satisfaction that pure capitalism could continue to grow in a completely capitalist world. What would be the continuing inducement to invest? Where would the demand come from to sustain the new investment? The problem was 'overproduction' or 'underconsumption': how could capitalists continue to invest in production when profitable markets for these goods might not exist? The answer to this question became her best known work, *The Accumulation of Capital.*

In Marx's view, capitalism, like all previous economic systems, contained the seeds of its own destruction. Capitalism must fail because of lack of demand, the drive for profits and the frenzied competition. Eventually a stream of goods would be produced for which there would be no purchasers. Workers would desire to purchase the products but would be unable to do so because of their low incomes. Capitalists could consume some of the surplus but their primary desire was to invest, to accumulate capital and raise profits. Investment in an ever accumulating stock of capital would be warranted only if there was an ever expanding market for the goods produced. Would capitalists continue to produce and invest if they could not sell their current output at a profit? Of course not. Competition and the drive for profits would cause repeated economic crises where small firms failed and more workers were laid off. The result was a falling profit rate, technological unemployment, class polarization, conflict and increasingly severe industrial crises. Eventually, one very large and final crisis would lead to the revolution. Ahead lay a new and more humane way of organizing economic life–socialism. Was this wrong? No, answered Luxemburg; it was just incomplete. Thus, *The Accumulation of Capital* was designed to finish and advance Marx's analysis.

The problem with Marx's work centred on investment – the accumulation of capital. Using numbers to describe behaviour in two sectors of the economy, Marx sought to prove that continual economic expansion could occur within a totally capitalist world even though there would be recurrent crises. In the arithmetic model that Marx used to make his points, very special assumptions had to be made to come to this conclusion; use of more probable values led to a different conclusion. Further, the question of effective demand for the goods that resulted from the increased productive capacity was left unanswered.

Luxemburg's answer was that capitalism survived by invading primitive economies – imperialism. To have continual accumulation of capital there must be 'a strata of buyers outside capitalist society'.[11] Luxemburg wrote, 'Imperialism is the political expression of the accumulation of capital in its competitive struggle for what remains still open of the non-capitalist environment'.[12] The advanced capitalist countries can survive only by exploiting the pre-capitalist countries. Through trade, conquest or trickery, they would export the economic crises. Colonies or even formally independent nations provide markets for the surplus goods produced at home while their own production is displaced. She wrote, 'Only the continuous and progressive disintegration of non-capitalist organizations makes accumulation of capital possible'.[13] India, for example, could absorb a very large amount of Britain's textiles but the household and village textile industries would be destroyed. Even more complex trade patterns could occur with not necessarily primitive but less developed countries, where profit rates would be higher than at home. The following might serve as an example:

> Cloth from Lancashire pays for labour in America, which is used to produce wheat and cotton. These provide wages and raw materials to the Lancashire mills, while the profits acquired both on the plantations and in the mills are invested in steel rails and rolling stock, which open up fresh territories so that the whole process is continuously expanding.[14]

Further, colonies could supply the imperialist country with otherwise unobtainable goods, rubber for example. This would increase profits and provide employment at home, as exploitation was exported to the rest of the world. Economic crises could be reduced in the mother country and capitalism would appear beneficial to both employers and workers.

Luxemburg held that the search for profitable markets would lead to repeated conflicts among the capitalist countries. Wars among the colonial powers raised profits and absorbed a good deal of production and this eliminated the surplus of goods that would otherwise occur. She explained, 'Capital[ism] increasingly employs militarism for implementing a foreign and colonial policy to get hold of the means of production and labour power of non-capitalist countries and societies'.[15] Yet the postponement of the ever threatening economic crises could not last forever. Unless profitable markets or wars could expand indefinitely, overproduction would return on a global scale. Luxemburg explained that the capitalist economy experiences a string of political and social disasters which lead to the revolution. She concluded:

> Capitalism is the first mode of economy with the weapon of propaganda, a mode which tends to engulf the entire globe and to stamp out all other economies, tolerating no rival at its side. Yet at the same time it is also the first mode of economy which is unable to exist by itself, which needs other economic systems as a medium and soil. Although it strives to become universal, and indeed, on account of this tendency, it must break down. . . .[16]

Hence, capitalism would crumble of its own weight; it would die of its internal contradictions as Marx predicted after all.

During the writing of *The Accumulation of Capital*, Rosa's tortuous affair with Leo Jogiches ended. As her power and influence had increased in the socialist movement, he stood more in her shadow. He was jealous of her success and she felt guilty; their relationship had become a psychic ballet of manipulation and guilt. Neither had been happy and there had been many clashes of their strong wills. Still, showing the strength she had built within herself, she continued her extremely active political life. It was her political activity, not her writings on economics, which landed her in jail.

Luxemburg hoped that war could be prevented by a mass refusal of workers to fight their socialist brothers in other countries. If a mobilization did start, she expected a mass strike and a refusal of workers to support imperialist aims. When the Kaiser and the government asked for war credits in 1914, Luxemburg thought that the German socialists in the Reichstag would vote against them. Events proved her wrong. All but one of the deputies were swept into the nationalist and patriotic tide to vote for the credits. Luxemburg was stunned. Nevertheless she continued to preach revolt, an end to the war, and international socialism. She continued to hope that workers around the world would understand the evil of capitalism and put an end to its rule. She became known to detractors as 'the Red Prima Donna' or 'the Jewish Rose' and was in danger of arrest and worse.

In early 1914, the feared arrest came after a speech in which she was accused of inciting soldiers to mutiny. What she actually said was, 'If they expect us to murder our French or other brothers, then let us tell them, "No, under no circumstances" '.[17] On another occasion she wrote, 'In the event of war breaking out . . . it is their [the workers'] duty to take measures to bring it to an end as quickly as possible, and to utilize the political crisis brought about by the war to arouse the masses of the people and accelerate the overthrow of capitalist class rule'.[18] To no one's surprise, she went to jail and was not freed until 1918.

With the fall of the Kaiser, Luxemburg was released and lost no time returning to her revolutionary activities. She spoke at rallies frequently and wrote of the choice between capitalism/barbarism and socialism – the salvation of humanity. Anything seemed possible in the chaos following the war; she urged workers to secure their future. The revolution might be at hand, and she warned workers that capitalists would fight to protect their property and politicians to preserve their power. The working class must hold on to any gains tenaciously and strengthen itself to fight off the inevitable backlash. Rosa knew that many revolutionaries were being arrested by supporters and police of the old regime. She too was being sought and colleagues recognized her life was in danger. While hiding in the apartment of a friend, she was arrested by a local para-military group and taken to the hotel that served as its headquarters. She was interrogated roughly and the order was given to take her by car to a civil prison nearby. As she was led to the car, one of the soldiers smashed her skull with two blows of his rifle butt. She was then dragged off to the waiting car, hit again and finished off with a shot to the head. Her corpse was thrown into a canal, where it was finally discovered months later.

Leo Jogiches, shocked by the murder of his former lover, investigated the crime. He managed to publish accounts of eyewitnesses and a photograph of the soldiers who committed the crime; they were said to be celebrating her death at the hotel where she had been questioned and abused.[19] That revelation probably resulted in his own arrest. At Police Headquarters, it was reported that he was 'shot to death trying to escape'.[20]

Three years after Rosa Luxemburg's murder, Lenin wrote about his revolutionary colleague, one with whom he had a number of disagreements. He commented with two lines from 'a good old Russian fable: an eagle can indeed sometimes fly lower than a chicken, but a chicken can never rise to the same heights as an eagle. Rosa Luxemburg erred on . . . But despite all these mistakes she was and remains an eagle'.[21]

In 1951, *The Accumulation of Capital* was published by the Yale University Press, with an introduction by Joan Robinson. After analysing the successive Marxist models by which Rosa Luxemburg had developed her thesis, Robinson rephrased the problem of accumulation in modern terms. The problem Luxemburg explored, she stated, is the inducement to invest. Robinson wrote that, 'Investment can take place in an ever-accumulating stock of capital only if the capitalists are assured of an ever expanding market for the goods which the capital will produce'.[22] Moreover, Robinson recognized that Rosa Luxemburg had provided a theory of the dynamic development of capitalism and, in doing so, was on the threshold of a more complete theory of investment.

Luxemburg bequeathed two legacies to the Marxist economists who followed her: she showed Marx's error in presenting his model of capital accumulation and she correctly described the relationship between capitalism and colonial expansion. Luxemburg's analysis of Marx's arithmetic examples proved that his conclusions depended on making very special assumptions and that there was no reason to believe that these circumstances would ever hold in actual situations. Her description of the relationship between the capitalist nations and the rest of the world was brilliant. That imperialism can sustain capitalism is shown very clearly.[23] How prescient she was when she wrote, 'Capital cannot accumulate without the aid of non-capitalist organizations, nor, on the other hand can it tolerate their continued existence side by side with itself. Only the continued progressive disintegration of non-capitalist organizations makes the accumulation of capital possible'.[24]

And what of Luxemburg's legacy to modern non-Marxist economists? First, she addressed the issue of the growth of effective demand, and she anticipated the growth models of the twentieth century. Second, she provided an excellent explanation of the hundred-year secular boom attributed to capitalist expansion around the world. The plantations, the railroads and perhaps the armed skirmishes would not have taken place if the pull of high profits had not motivated capitalist investors.

She also addressed the issue of the adequacy of effective demand. Secular stagnation, or the absence of effective demand has received considerable attention from twentieth century economists, and Luxemburg correctly pointed out that stagnation leads to collapse. Yet she failed to address the question of the equality of savings and investment. That was left to Keynes, who lectured readers that savings must equal investment in his *General Theory*.

Luxemburg opposed World War I and founded the German Communist Party. She proved to many that the end of the capitalist social order was inevitable. She was an inspiration to revolutionaries and opposed all compromise with capitalist governments. In Germany and other countries her work is studied by historians of socialism and anti-militarists. In the 1960s and 1970s her picture was carried in parades by student demonstrators to whom her support for democracy appealed.[25] Yet, after more than seven decades, her writings still have opponents. In 1972 the West German government created an uproar by issuing a stamp with her likeness, as some individuals refused to accept the letters that bore it.[26] Whether loved or hated, she could not be ignored.

Notes

1. Nettl, J.P. (1966), *Rosa Luxemburg*, 2 vols, London: Oxford University Press, vol. 1, p. 55.
2. Nettl (1966), vol. 1, p. 57.
3. Frolich, Paul (1972), *Rosa Luxemburg: Her Life and work*, first published in English 1940, New York and London: Monthly Review Press, p. 6.
4. Nettl (1966), vol. 1, p. 59.
5. Nettl (1966), vol. 1, p. 59.
6. Ettinger, E. (ed.), (1979), *Comrade and Lover: Rosa Luxemburg's Letters to Leo Jogiches*, Cambridge, MA: Massachusetts Institute of Technology Press, p. 27.
7. Ettinger (1979), p. 28.
8. Luxemburg, Rosa (1899), *Sozialreform oder Revolution (Social Reform or Revolution)*, Leipzig (2nd edn 1908), quoted from Mary-Alice Waters. (1970) *Rosa Luxemburg Speaks*, New York: Pathfinder Press, pp. 33–90.
9. Luxemburg, Rosa, *Introduction to Political Economy*. Never published in complete form. It was published in partial form in 1925, Paul Levi, (ed.) Berlin.
10. Quoted from Frolich (1972), p. 130.
11. Luxemburg, Rosa (1951) *The Accumulation of Capital*, originally published in German [1913], London: Routledge and Kegan Paul, p. 351.
12. Luxemburg (1951), p. 446.
13. Luxemburg (1951), p. 416.
14. Robinson, Joan, introduction to Luxemburg (1951), p. 27.
15. Luxemburg (1951), p. 466.
16. Luxemburg (1951), p. 467.
17. Cliff, Tony (1959), *Rosa Luxemburg*, published as numbers 2 and 3 of *International Socialism*, quarterly journal for Marxist Theory, p. 16.
18. Cliff (1959), pp. 33–4.
19. Frolich, (1972), p. 301. The photograph is contained in Nettl (1966) vol. 2, p. 762.
20. Frolich, (1972), p. 301.
21. *Pravda*, 1924; Quoted in Frolich, (1972), p. 304.
22. Luxemburg (1951), p. 21.
23. Her conclusions follow logically if the investment schedule is steep. If, however, rising real income is allowed for workers, then different results can be obtained.
24. Luxemburg (1951), p. 416.
25. She valued freedom but spent substantial time in jail. She wrote so passionately and clearly of the value of freedom that German school children are sometimes taught phrases from her work. In fact Chancellor Helmut Kohl inadvertently quoted one of these maxims. What Luxemburg wrote was 'Freedom only for the supporters of

the government, only for the members of the Party, no matter how numerous they may be, is no freedom at all'. Quoted from Daniel Egger's review of Margarethe von Trotta's film on Luxemburg, *The Nation*, 25 April 1987, **244**, p. 546.

26. Egger, 1987, p. 546.

5 Beatrice Webb (1858–1943)

The fifth of Adam Smith's intellectual daughters, Beatrice Potter Webb, was a prolific writer whose successes received great public attention. British socialism, implemented by the Labour Party after World War II, is greatly indebted to her for its basic premises. She rejected both the classical economic thought embraced by Marcet, Martineau and Fawcett and also the Marxist economics of Rosa Luxemburg. She developed her own philosophical synthesis of democratic collectivism in social organization.

To appreciate fully the contribution of Beatrice Webb to economics and to the study of society, it is necessary to examine briefly the economic issues current in Britain at the midpoint of the nineteenth century, particularly that of income distribution. The Industrial Revolution that had brought much benefit to the nation had also brought a sharp division of living standards experienced by the highest and lowest classes of the population. At the extremes were the successful capitalists, who enjoyed luxury previously unknown by their earlier counterparts; at the other extreme were the workers displaced from the countryside and living near the many factories where they found employment. Beatrice Webb, writing at a time when she was studying the roots of social institutions, described the situation: 'Mobs of starving factory hands paraded the manufacturing towns; secret societies honeycombed with sedition and conspiracy sprang up with amazing rapidity among the better paid artisans[1]'. As economic and social changes occurred, political change also took place. Political power was transferred from the rural aristocracy to the middle class, to the capitalist-entrepreneurs. The result was a pyramiding of material wealth that, in a period of unprecedented national prosperity, left 30 per cent of the inhabitants of London in destitution and chronic poverty.[2]

The capitalists – merchants and manufacturers – were understandably proud of their accomplishments. They pointed to the rapidly increasing production of goods, the opportunities for personal profits, and the accumulation of property as proofs that the *laissez-faire* system was successful. They found satisfaction in the fact that Britain, by becoming the workshop of the world, had become prosperous. They overlooked, or thought inevitable, the accompanying conditions of unemployment, poverty and malnutrition. Further, they held to a rather libertarian interpretation of the Smith–Malthus–Ricardo doctrine of *laissez-faire* and were largely complacent in the face of society's ills. For the most part, they believed that poverty was a man's own fault and should be treated as a crime, with every man left to suffer the consequences of his own action. Three broad themes were repeated: people should work harder; only the lazy and incompetent were poor; and persistent effort on the part of the indigent would yield a better civilization. These ideas were dominant in the economic philosophy of Victorian England.

On the other hand were social critics and reformers, to which the voice of Beatrice Webb was eventually added. These included evolutionary socialists, typified earlier by Robert Owen, and the revolutionary socialists such as Marx. They were united in one belief that the meaning of progress was more than the accumulation of wealth by a relative few; instead they defined progress as a more equitable distribution of the fruits of economic growth.

The capitalists were frightened at the prospect of a violent revolution deposing the established order or of having to tax themselves in order to provide for those less fortunate than they were. At this point it seemed that the capitalist-individualists and the revolutionary socialists were bound on a collision course that could lead to open conflict. However, during the latter half of the nineteenth century, England possessed a group of intellectuals, of whom Beatrice Webb was a prominent member, who realized that a compromise between the two factions had to be reached in order to avoid a senseless upheaval. They sought to propagate a philosophy that would draw out the best principles of both groups. Beatrice Webb's share in accomplishing this synthesis constituted her not-inconsiderable contribution to society.

Beatrice Potter Webb was born Beatrice Potter on 2 January 1858 at Standish House, near Gloucester, to Richard and Lawrencia Potter. Her father was a successful, gregarious mid-Victorian businessman and railroad magnate, her mother a beautiful, restless, intelligent woman. Eighth of nine daughters, Beatrice was neglected for not being male and instead was simply accepted into the growing brood. When Beatrice was four, a male child, Dicky, was born who took centre stage as the long-awaited son. Subsequently Beatrice's needs, even as a young child, were frequently ignored. In her diary, Potter writes of being thrown out of the nursery one morning completely naked, because the nurse was too busy to attend to a four-year-old girl's buttons and bows.[3]

Being one of many, Beatrice was often left alone to entertain herself. Any attempts her parents made at establishing her studies were to no avail; Beatrice refused to be shut up inside to study, much preferring to explore the surrounding grounds of the Cotswold hills. Her mother

Lawrencia dismissed the child as being dim-witted, writing, 'Beatrice is the only one of my children who is below the average in intelligence'.[4]

When Dicky died at age two, Lawrencia's involvement with her children became even more infrequent. She developed into a recluse, and Richard's involvement in the Great Western Railway and his partnership in a prosperous timber business left little time to concern himself with the children. Beatrice later recalled her childhood as 'creeping in the shadow of my baby brother's birth and death'.[5]

Beatrice's only solace came from a distant female relative and companion to Lawrencia, 'Dada'. Dada governed the entire household, nurturing the children and even speaking up for them when they were in disgrace. From Dada Beatrice learned the importance of love, which she bestowed upon any person in need. Beatrice later wrote of the nurse, 'Dada was a saint, the only saint I ever knew . . . she mothered all the members of the large household, whether children or servants, whether good or naughty; she nursed them when they were ill, comforted them when they were in trouble, and spoke for them when they were in disgrace.[6]

With so little communication with other people, Beatrice's isolation deepened into a psychosomatic sickliness. She was plagued by minor ailments, nervous headaches, and neuralgia. Frequently she was depressed. At the age of 14 she began to keep a regular diary (a practice she would continue until her death) in which she found some therapeutic comfort from her frustrations. She considered suicide, imagining marvellous scenes of repentance, and went so far as to hide chloroform. She began to search for meaning in religion, studying Catholicism, Buddhism, Judaism and the 'Religion of Humanity'; she read the Bible and Plato, translated Faust and took up spiritualism. She wanted to find something that would explain her suffering, a religion immersed in an unselfish demand for the highest duties. Although she never attached her beliefs to any particular sect, she began to develop a moral code of her own.

Beatrice was encouraged by her father to take her educational pursuits seriously. One of the results of his encouragement was her introduction at the age of 19 to a friend of the family, popular philosopher and sociologist Herbert Spencer. He became her intellectual confidant, taking her for long walks during which he would explain evolution and philosophy. Part of that religion she was searching for was satisfied in his evolutionary theory of society. From him she discovered the importance of a scientific method of reasoning, later writing, 'What he taught me to discern was not the truth, but the relevance of facts'.[7]

Beatrice also became caught up in the Potter daughters' society life. It was said that a successful debut for a girl was as important as a university education for a male child, as 'marriage to a man of their own or a higher social grade was the only recognized vocation for women not compelled to earn their own livelihood'.[8]

Characteristically Lawrencia did not attend to her daughters' coming out and left them to find husbands on their own. Beatrice was dragged along by her sisters to all of the London summer season dances and saw them married off to successful young men year after year. Although she was enticed by the romantic engagements and excited by the frivolity, her high sense of moral purpose left her feeling guilty. She made up for these periods of opulence by returning to her studies in full force over the winters, suffering again from psychosomatic bouts of depression. Her frustrations were somewhat reduced by a late-founded friendship with her sister Maggie, but that was cut short by Maggie's marriage.

Beatrice travelled extensively throughout Europe with her sisters' new families in order to get away from the rapidly shrinking Potter family. She performed her family responsibilities, dutifully entertaining for her industrious father and caring for her younger sister Rosy (whose curse of being closest to the dead Dicky in age, made her rejection from Lawrencia the most severe).

Without any close friendships or close connections to family members, and with increasing responsibilities to the family as the oldest unwed daughter, Beatrice became very independent. Her imagination soared while she searched for the answers to all of her questions. Her study convinced her that social ills could be discovered by fact finding and cured by recommendations for reform based on scientific examination. She decided that the scientific investigation of social institutions was to be her vocation in life. It was the calling which was to motivate the rest of her life, to become a social investigator and to increase the well-being of the whole society.

As Beatrice's responsibilities as the caretaker of the Potter family grew, she began to empathize with her mother Lawrencia. She too was an educated woman with ambitions that were left unfulfilled as a result of marriage. Like Beatrice, Lawrencia's depression led her into a religiously zealous life in which she preferred prayer to familial ties. The mutual understanding of mother and daughter led them to grow closer, Lawrencia taking back some of her previous prejudices. After they learned to communicate effectively, their friendship grew; unfortunately, Lawrencia died soon after in 1882.

With her mother gone, Beatrice became the official head of the family. She turned once again toward religion and vowed to give up her academic studies, hoping to gain more understanding from her family. Alas, giving up her studies proved impossible. Instead she got into the habit of waking early in the morning in order to squeeze in three extra hours of study. Her newly found busyness did help to lift her depression and she became more energetic, more sociable and less inclined to self-criticism.

After months of being trapped at home, Beatrice regained her interest in events outside of the Potter home. She took up reading about political science in an attempt to work out in her own mind what were the 'imbalances of society'.[9] Desperate to begin her career of social investigation, she finally convinced her father to send Rosy off to boarding school. Beatrice then moved to London and joined Octavia Hill's Charity Organization Society (COS). Her task was to screen those worthy of receiving aid. She wrote that, 'the C.O.S. appeared to me an honest . . . attempt to apply the scientific method of observation and experiment . . . to the task of delivering the poor from their miseries'.[10]

In 1883, Beatrice fell in love. Joseph Chamberlain, the most influential and brilliant radical politician of his day, was 47, twice widowed and handsome. His recent reorganization of the Liberal Party made him the new leader of the growing radical elements in the party. Beatrice was immediately attracted to him, and it was fairly obvious that he was to her, but she hesitated at his radicalism. She soon realized that marriage to such a powerful man would mean a compromise of her own desires. Through discussions of politics, Beatrice realized that Chamberlain wanted a helpmate while she wanted a husband who would consider her an intellectual equal. Many of the Potter family were also hesitant about his radicalism, but they strongly approved of his eligibility. As one of the most powerful men of his time, Chamberlain would have been a very good catch for one of the Potter daughters. When he seemed less interested in her, Beatrice returned to her studies.

In 1883 Beatrice concluded that a study of science was necessary for understanding society. After some tutoring by one of her brothers-in-law in biology, she gave up the 'hard' sciences from boredom. Instead she resolved to pursue what are now the 'social sciences' deciding to begin her investigations with a real world situation.

Beatrice began by asking her old nurse Dada to allow her to join a visit to her relations in Bacup, a cotton mill town in Lancashire. Disguising herself as a Welsh farmer's daughter, 'Miss Jones', Beatrice spent a few weeks living as a member of the working class. She acquired a great respect for the warmth and honesty of ordinary people. She also saw the benefit yielded by the Factory Acts and she wrote, '*Laissez-*

faire breaks down when one watches these things from the inside'.[11] This visit was to influence her thinking a great deal, for it was there that she found much value in the Co-operative Movement, an institution she was to support throughout her life. She continued to consider whether it might be possible to eliminate poverty, instead of just alleviating it.

After the visit Beatrice returned to London and went to work as a rent collector for Octavia Hill's charitable housing schemes. Becoming the landlady for the St Katherine's Buildings, a group of tenements constructed to provide adequate housing for deserving families, Beatrice came in direct contact with the urban poor for the first time. She was appalled at the conditions and offended at the inhabitants' apparent lack of morality. She found that what little help was offered to the poor was fragmented and inefficient and she proposed collecting the data and pooling the resources of all of the agencies involved.

Beatrice still had her familial responsibilities. In 1885, Beatrice's father suffered a stroke that paralysed him. Beatrice's personal interests had to be set aside. As the oldest unmarried daughter she feared the prospect of being chained to her father's bedside. Her depression returned. In her diary she wrote, 'If Death comes it will be welcome, for life has always been distasteful'.[12] While at home Beatrice continued her involvement with poor relief by writing a letter to the Pall Mall Gazette that became an article titled 'A Lady's View of the Unemployed'. In it, she argued against setting up relief work in the poor district of London (the East End) because it would attract more people to an area with a scarcity of jobs already. She noted the article's publication as 'a turning point in my life'.[13] The article caught the attention of her cousin by marriage, Charles Booth, who had begun work on a monumental study, *Inquiry into the Life and Labour of the People of London*. Booth asked Beatrice to help him with his project.

Charles Booth was one of the first nineteenth century social investigators to use the scientific method in social investigation. He sought to discover what were the real facts of the lives of the poor. This was an intellectual position and an area of interest that suited Beatrice well, and she joined the project as 'an industrious apprentice.' Both she and Booth believed that political economy as it was currently understood failed 'from want of reality'[14] and that this deficiency could be remedied only by direct study of people's behaviour. He expected his investigations to disprove the socialists' contention that 25 per cent of wage earners were paid insufficient amounts to maintain physical health. His research, in fact, revealed that more than 30 per cent of wage earners were living in a state of chronic destitution or on the edge of bare subsistence.[15] The entire Booth inquiry, begun in 1886, resulted in 17 volumes, publication of which extended over 17 years.

Beatrice's first recognition as a social investigator came in 1887 when she published the results of her investigation for the Booth project, an article titled 'The Dock Life of East London' which appeared in the leading review *Nineteenth Century*.[16] In addition to helping her to acquire confidence in her ability to do the work she believed in, the Booth inquiry had contributed to her intellectual growth in two ways: first, by pointing to the right relation between personal observation and statistical method; and second, by causing her to become aware of the importance of the trade union movement, which was to play an important role in her professional career. By 1890 Beatrice Potter had become established as a progressive intellectual.

All the while Beatrice was still dealing with her feelings for Joseph Chamberlain. Her increased activity in intellectual circles made their meetings more frequent and their apparent fondness for each other more established. Beatrice attempted to draw him closer; after several uneventful meetings and with no progress in sight, she became bold. She wrote a very direct letter to him expressing her feelings. Instead of indicating similar sentiments Chamberlain claimed confusion, stating that he had never had such feelings for her and he did not want this to ruin their friendship. Beatrice was mortified and feared she would never love again. She took refuge in her research.

Her next investigative project was the East End tailoring trade's 'sweating system', a putting out system where workers were paid a small amount per piece completed. In order to get local colour and to gain insight into the organization of a workshop, she worked in disguise in 1887 as an operator, a plain trouser hand, in several workshops. In 1890, her articles appeared as 'The Tailoring Trade of East London'. This was followed by 'Pages from a Work-girl's Diary'. Subsequently she was called upon to give evidence to the Lord's Committee on the Sweating System. To the question 'How would you define the Sweating System?' asked by a member of the Lord's Committee, she answered: 'An enquiry into the Sweating System is practically an enquiry into all labour employed in manufacture which has escaped the regulation of the Factory Act and trade unions'.[17] To this, she added that the workers are 'oppressed and defrauded in every aspect of their lives'; they were exploited by shopkeepers, by landlords and by 'every man, woman, and child who consumes the product of their labour'.[18]

The philosophy of universality of responsibility for social ills contained in this statement was repeated years later when, upon being asked by another national committee to explain exactly what was meant by destitution, she replied, 'destitution is a disease of society itself'.[19] It was evident by 1890 that Beatrice was moving with increasing confidence into the path of her career. She was seeing social problems in ever larger focus and was being accepted in her own right as an authority on social conditions.

Fulfilled professionally, Beatrice was still lonely. Rosy was married and, at the age of 30, Beatrice was the last unwed Potter girl. She soon resigned herself to becoming an old maid. She found fulfilment in her work and was continually receiving invitations for work and presentations. Satisfied with her situation, she actually became happy for a time. When Chamberlain announced his engagement to a young American girl, she was reminded of her previous dreams and her depression returned. Yet after this marriage she was finally able to put him and the six years she had spent in love with him behind her.

Beatrice was happy with her success in writing but horrified by her in-depth experiences with the poor. As a result she came to question her previous economic beliefs. Finally rejecting Spencer's Social Darwinist approach, Beatrice decided to investigate further the possibilities offered by the cooperative movement. In preparation she studied the history and theory of cooperation and attended Cooperative Congresses. She now felt that the answer to the poverty question lay in a society based on self-governing workshops that would enable workers to own their own capital, thus eliminating the capitalist entrepreneur. She saw cooperation 'as one form of democratic association, as one aspect of that larger movement towards an Industrial Democracy which has characterized the history of the British working class of the nineteenth century'.[20] She set about putting her thoughts on paper. After describing the condition of the working class, she outlined the essential principles of consumer and producer cooperation as a form of economic organization. In 1891 Potter's detailed 250-page book was published as *The Cooperative Movement in Great Britain.*

During this time Beatrice was uninterested in the concurrent suffrage movement. In fact she had gone so far as to sign a famous anti-suffrage manifesto written by the novelist Mrs Humphrey Ward. Millicent Fawcett, who supported suffrage for women, was infuriated by Beatrice's decision. Beatrice herself was to regret the endorsement for most of the rest of her life, recanting it 20 years later. Her reasons for signing were complex: she was still highly influenced by Spencer's theories of social evolution; she had no interest in politics beyond social reform and found no need to vote; and, most important, as a wealthy intellectual Beatrice had never been discriminated against herself.

In March of 1889, Beatrice's father had another stroke, once again tying her to his bedside. She became lonely, longing for companionship. Spinsterhood seemed a deep burden. She wrote, 'God knows celibacy is as painful to a woman (even from the physical standpoint) as it is to a man – It could not be more painful than it is to woman'.[21] To lessen her isolation she turned to the study of political economy.

Beatrice undertook the study without enthusiasm, and recorded, 'Political economy is hateful – most hateful drudgery. Still, it is evident to me I must master it.'[22] Her study culminated in two essays 'The History of English Economics', and 'The Economic Theory of Karl Marx'. The first of these took the form of a series of notes, 'On the Nature of Economic Science', the substance of which appeared much later as an appendix to her first autobiographical volume, *My Apprenticeship*. In the essay she sought 'to understand what are in fact the data upon which political economy is based – what are its necessary assumptions'.[23] It provides us with perhaps our best insight into Beatrice Webb, the economist. After concluding her studies in early 1887, she recognized that she had been carried out of her depth as a reasoner and she had come to doubt 'the desirability of a water-tight science of political economy'.[24] She viewed the sphere of economics as involving studies in social pathology and concluded that political economy should be treated not as a self-contained, separate, abstract subject but as a branch of an all-embracing study of human behaviour in society and of social institutions.

Pursuing this interdisciplinary view, she suggested, 'Assuming that we give up the conception of a separate abstract science of Political Economy or Economics, the adjective "economic" might then be reserved to define the relations between men arising out of their means of livelihood or subsistence.'[25] She elaborated this idea by suggesting that economics should be studied as an evolving organism:

> not in any assumed perfection of development, but in all the changing phases of growing social tissue from embryo to corpse, in health and perversion, in short, as the birth, growth, disease and death of actual social relationships. And their diseases may even be the most interesting part of the study.[26]

She also considered the subject of value in economics; that is, the reason that goods trade at the relative prices that they do. Here she cites Karl Marx and declares the inadequacy of his labour theory of value, writing:

> According to his theory of value, economic faculty, or as he preferred to call it, 'labor', is the sole origin of value; he assumed that economic desire is, like the ether, always present; and can therefore be neglected as a joint parent

> of value.... To read Marx, one would think that it was only necessary to make a yard of cloth in order to create exchange value to the cost of production, together with a handsome surplus.![27]

She called the Marxist world 'weird' where 'men are automata, commodities have souls; money is incarnated life, and capital has a life-process of its own!' And she added, 'This idea of an "automaton owner", thus making profit without even being conscious of the existence of any desire to be satisfied, is, to any one who has lived with financial or industrial undertakings, in its glaring discrepancy with facts, nothing less than grotesque'.[28]

In the course of this research, and upon introspective reflection, Beatrice realized that she had become a socialist. She had arrived there in recognizable stages, after initial resistance. The conversion had begun in fact in 1883 during her visit to the Lancashire cotton mills, when she gained new respect for the Factory Acts and the role of government in their enforcement. Gradually she became convinced that it was impossible to improve the lot of the poor merely by exhortation or entreaty of the industrialists or the workers. From her investigation of the sweated industries she had concluded that sweating occurred as a consequence of allowing uncontrolled free competition under capitalism in any industry that could escape the regulations of the Factory Act and the trade unions. This she identified as Stage I of her conversion to socialism. After she could see no way out of the recurrent periods of inflation and depression, with the view that the regime of private property could not withstand revolution, she arrived at Stage II on her road to socialism. She wrote, 'This "national minimum" of civilized existence, to be legally ensured for every citizen, was the second stage in my progress towards socialism'.[29] She came to believe that industry had first to be governed by 'democracies of consumers' and later by 'democracies of workers'. Thus, she gained the conviction that collective governance was the only way to advance the common good and eliminate class prerogatives and sectional interests. She wrote, 'only under the communal ownership of the means of production, can you arrive at the most perfect form of individual development... in other words complete socialism is only consistent with absolute individualism'.[30] As a result of her investigations, Beatrice embraced socialist principles based on ethics and morality and celebrated, 'At last I am a Socialist!'[31]

Another result of her studies was her introduction to Sidney Webb in 1890. Webb was a London civil servant, one of the leaders of the Progressive party and a leader of the Fabian Society. Beatrice and Sidney had read some of the other's work admiringly before they met, and Beatrice was particularly impressed with Webb's *Fabian Essays in Socialism.* Sidney made himself immediately useful to Beatrice by providing research and advice on her studies while her father remained ill.

On a professional level their interests were well matched, but this was not so on a personal level. Sidney quickly fell in love with Beatrice. Sidney, Beatrice thought, was ugly with '. . . a huge head on a very tiny body'.[32]

Although not attracted to him, Beatrice was certainly flattered by his attention towards her and impressed with his intelligence and work. Sidney attempted to get closer to her by begging for help with a paper on old age pensions and the Poor Law. He also volunteered to attend a meeting of the Co-operative Congress in Glasgow with her. It was in Glasgow that Sidney professed his love for Beatrice, a confession she did not welcome. Like Chamberlain's response to Beatrice's letter, her response to Sidney's disclosure was merely a hope for continued friendship. As Sidney continued the pursuit, Beatrice became increasingly distant. She asked that he think of her as a married woman and warned that, if he even reached for her hand, their friendship was off. Sidney wrote in his first love letter:

> Because I am through and through yours already. . . . I could be as great an adjunct to your intellectual life as you are to my moral being. Of course, I stand to gain by far the most, because I gain your intellect too, and cannot give you moral help. *But together we could move the world.*[33]

Beatrice immediately made it clear that she wished to receive no more personal sentiments. Of course Sidney could not keep his feelings to himself. He furthered Beatrice's anger as he read Keats and Rossetti to her. He wrote more love letters, to which Beatrice replied that he was not being considerate of her feelings. Finally, when regrets about her harshness led Beatrice to return to Sidney, she asked for advice on a book on Cooperation that a publisher had requested her to write (on Sidney's suggestion).

Their friendship and working relationships were renewed. Beatrice gradually became part of Sidney's circle of friends, the Fabians, of which she commented, 'What charms me is the perfect sort of relationship between your little knot of men – it is singularly trustful; you really care for each other. Such friendship is very precious, it defies cynicism'.[34]

Given her failed relationship with Chamberlain, Beatrice feared becoming involved with another man. She felt she must explain this to Sidney, writing:

> I cannot and will not be engaged to you. . . . Dear Sidney, I will try to love you, but don't be impatient. . . . I am doing more than I would do for any other man simply because you are a Socialist and I am a Socialist. That other man I loved but did not believe in, you I believe in but do not love. Will it end equally unhappily?'[35]

Yet she was already attached to Sidney and depended on his support in her work.

In November 1890 Sidney became very ill with scarlet fever. He considered with despair the state of his relationship with Beatrice and resolved that his wishes would never be fulfilled. He wrote to her of his feelings one last time, and she again rejected him. She responded,

> To be perfectly frank I did at one time fancy I was beginning to care for you but. . . . I do not believe my nature is capable of love. And this being the case – the fact that I do not love you – cannot, and will never, make the stupendous sacrifice of marriage.[36]

They agreed to continue as friends, and Beatrice drew up careful guidelines for their friendship. Beatrice joined the Fabian Society officially under the condition that only her initials be published in the list of members. Sidney considered leaving the Colonial office and running for Parliament or the London County Council. Beatrice advised him to stay with his present position and he harshly criticized her work on the Cooperation book. Beatrice was asked to give several lectures on the Cooperative Movement and nervous about her first lecture, she asked Sidney to help by drafting a press release about it. Sidney summarized her lecture and Beatrice was amazed at his apparent ease with the subject.

Beatrice was beginning to falter in her previous distance from Sidney. It could have been the very fact that he appeared to be getting along without her, or her nervousness and self-doubt about becoming a distinguished intellectual, or simply her fear of just being alone. During the Cooperative Congress in May, Beatrice admitted that she loved Sidney in return. The two became secretly engaged, in order not to anger her father. Beatrice wrote in her diary, 'I am not "in love", not as I was . . . our marriage will be based on fellowship – the common faith and a common work'.[37]

It was resolved that Sidney would retire from the Colonial Office to run for the London County Council. Together they would work on their trade union books. Beatrice feared the negative effect their relationship might have on her work, writing to Sidney, 'I love you – but I love my work better!'[38] They began work interviewing local trade unionists throughout the Northeast but when Sidney began running as the Progressive candidate for Deptford for the LCC, Beatrice was left alone to care for her father and continue the overwhelming work. While alone in the Northeast, Beatrice happened upon Chamberlain and his new American bride on a train. This meeting convinced her that she did not want to live the role of wife to Chamberlain as she saw how dependent and sheltered the bride appeared.

Beatrice's father died that New Year's Eve, leaving her free to marry. Beatrice immediately announced the engagement to her sisters. Worried about their reactions, she was relieved when they acted 'with tolerance and good sense'.[39] Although Sidney was below the family standard of means and position, his character and intelligence made him worthy of the Potter family. It was Herbert Spencer who refused his blessing of the marriage; he objected to Beatrice's marriage to someone who believed in the collectivist state.

After a spring of book research, political campaigning and meeting each other's families, Beatrice and Sidney were married on 23 July 1892. Beatrice marked the occasion in her diary with, 'exit Beatrice Potter, enter Beatrice Webb or rather (Mrs) Sidney Webb for I lose, alas, both names.'[40] Their honeymoon was spent in Dublin – another working vacation.

Thereafter their careers were combined: politically, through Sidney's 18 years of administrative service on the London County Council and Beatrice's membership on several governmental committees; intellectually, through their systematic research and voluminous publications. Their natures and talents supplemented each other's in countless ways. Sidney possessed a unique ability for research and writing; Beatrice had unlimited patience and zeal for the study of social institutions and for interviewing their leaders. Both researchers 'were democratic collectivists, believing in the eventual triumph, in so far as social environment is concerned, of the principle of equality between man and man'.[41] Together they pursued the course that Beatrice had set for herself: studies first in trade unionism, then in local government; and thereafter in poverty.

The first literary output of the Webb 'partnership' was *The History of Trade Unionism*, published in the Spring of 1894. This was a meticulous 800-page record of the origin and growth of the trade union movement from its earliest beginnings in Great Britain. The authors saw themselves as guardians of social history as they investigated the confidential records of some of the ancient local societies, convinced 'that the Trade Union records contain material of the utmost value to the future historian of industrial and political organization, and that these records are fast disappearing'.[42] This volume was, in fact, a historical introduction to their more ambitious study, *Industrial Democracy*, published in 1898, in which they developed their own theory of trade unionism with 'a new view of democracy' and 'an original set of economic and political hypotheses'.[43]

Industrial Democracy was well received upon publication and is particularly valued now by students of labour economics. The 900-page book was organized in three parts: trade union structure, four chapters; trade union function, thirteen chapters; trade union theory, four chapters; and four appendices. In this volume they examined the defects of the wage fund theory, which, with its opposition to trade unionism, had prevailed from 1825 to 1875. Thereafter the authors described their vision that trade unionism should, with technically trained leadership and responsible collective bargaining, assume a special function in the administration of industry in a democratic state, becoming the civil servant of public welfare. They wrote:

> Thus we arrive at the characteristic device of the Doctrine of a Living Wage, which we have termed the National Minimum – the deliberate enforcement, by an elaborate Labor Code, of a definite quota of education, sanitation, leisure, and wages for every grade of workers in every industry. This National Minimum the public opinion of the democratic state will not only support, but positively insist on for the common weal.[44]

The National Minimum became a theme central to all of their subsequent research, publications and policy objectives.

From their study of trade unionism the Webbs developed a new view of democracy. This new view propelled them into the study of English local government, where they hoped to discover, by studying structure, function and social environment, the source of compulsory collective action which might provide the mechanism for developing a socialist state. It was Sidney's zeal for discovering the means by which administrative efficiency in government might be best achieved that set the tone for their work.

Their research resulted in seven volumes, which were published between 1906 and 1929. Four volumes that appeared before 1920 described the development of English local government from the Revolution of 1688 to 1835 and dealt with the origins of parish, county, manor, borough, and special governmental authorities – an 'internal history of the eighteenth century'.[45] These were followed, starting in 1925 by three volumes on the history of the English Poor Law of 1834 and by publication of a number of studies on related topics.

During this 23-year interval, the Webbs were occupied by two other interests, economic education and economic policy. They were instrumental in establishing the London School of Economics and Political Science, which opened in 1895, and which Beatrice regarded as 'perhaps the biggest single enterprise in Our Partnership'.[46]

In February 1900 she recorded in her diary:

> Best of all [Sidney] has persuaded the Royal Commission to recognize economics as a science and not merely as a subject in the Arts Faculty. We have always claimed that the study of the structure and function of society was as much a science as the study of any other form of life, and ought to be pursued by the scientific methods used in other organic sciences. Such history as will be taught at the School will be the history of social institutions discovered from documents, statistics and the observation of the actual structure and working of living organizations. . . .[47]

Decisions on behalf of the School, its finances, its philosophy, its administration and faculty, as well as student conferences and their own lectures occupied the years that followed.

The Fabian Society was their second major interest. Beatrice had joined in 1892; Sidney had been a member since 1885, shortly after the society was founded. They, along with the mercurial George Bernard Shaw, the political theorist Graham Wallas and others, set its policies. Some of their views reflected those of John Stuart Mill who had bridged the gap between Benthamism and socialism. Fabian doctrine espoused a philosophy of gradualism as it sought to permeate existing society with collectivist ideals. 'Their summary of Socialism,' Beatrice wrote, 'comprised essentially collective ownership wherever practicable; collective regulation everywhere else; collective provision according to need for all the impotent and sufferers; and collective taxation in proportion to wealth, especially surplus wealth'.[48]

In November 1905 Beatrice was appointed a member of the Royal Commission on the Poor Law and the Relief of Distress. Although the appointment meant three years of intensive effort for her, it also gave her the opportunity to study the chronic destitution of whole sections of the people with whom she had not previously had contact. Beatrice was intent on investigating the causes and hence the means of preventing destitution, not on just developing methods of welfare relief. This commission appointment gave her the opportunity to put forth the Webbs' idea of a 'minimum standard of life', the forerunner of today's guaranteed annual income. This, they had determined, would include a national system of old-age pensions to be administered free from any stigma of pauperism, a provision for medical relief to be handled by the public health authorities; and a programme for the 'social disease of unemployment' that would involve an increase in the personal responsibility of the beneficiaries – the first blueprint of cradle-to-grave social security to be implemented within the existing social order.

The Commission's two reports, one by the commission's majority, the other a minority report (a joint project of the Webbs) were published in January 1909. Beatrice described the goals set forth in the Minority Report:

> . . . to secure a national minimum of civilized life . . . open to all alike, of both sexes and all classes, by which we meant sufficient nourishment and training when young, a living wage when able-bodied, treatment when sick, and a modest but secure livelihood when disabled or aged.[49]

This doctrine of a national minimum in income, health, housing, leisure, and education, was later cited in 1942 by Lord Beveridge, the author of the famed Beveridge Report, as 'the principal Webb contribution to social thought'.[50] For her work on the Poor Law Commission, Beatrice was awarded the degree of Doctor of Letters by Manchester University in July 1909.

The Webbs proposed to convert the nation to a policy of complete communal responsibility for the prevention of mass destitution in all forms, whether due to childhood, old age, sickness, illiteracy or unemployment. In order to publicize the message of the Minority Report and to create an awareness of the need for 'levelling up the bottomest layer of society'[51] the Webbs established the National Committee for the Prevention of Destitution. Their efforts proved successful, as the Minority Report Campaign generated a belief that society could be spared the vicious circle of degrading poverty by reorganizing the welfare services as established by the Poor Law of 1834. The Webbs saw destitution as 'a disease of society itself' and after gathering all available facts by which they could identify a 'poverty line', they proposed to convert Britain to a policy of complete communal responsibility for the prevention of mass destitution in all its forms. The campaign was 'to *really change* the mind of the people with regard to the facts of destitution'.[52] The campaign generated venomous controversy between those who would perpetuate the status quo and the supporters of the Webbs. Those who attacked their ideas tried to discredit the Webbs by demanding Sidney's resignation of the chairmanship of the London School of Economics.

The School was the Webbs' cherished educational institution. It had become their dearest 'child,' and this was an attack 'below the belt'. Beatrice wrote:

> It is an awkward corner to turn. We *do* value our connection, and *authoritative* connection with the School, and if Sidney were to retire presently from the chairmanship it would endanger the tie. On the other hand we value more the continued prosperity of the School so long as it remains unbiased and open to collectivist tendencies.[53]

The episode was resolved without damage to the school but the experience convinced the Webbs that it was necessary for them 'to drop into the background in the school's life'.[54] This they did after 1911, 'with placid content', but Sidney continued to support the school's library and endowment.

On 1 December 1912 Beatrice Webb wrote in her diary: 'Clifton. St Vincent's Hotel. Down here for a conference and public meeting on "War against Poverty". . . .' (This is probably the first use of this now familiar phrase. It appears in Webb's diary on several subsequent dates as she reports the progress of efforts to publicize the crusade for their national minimum of civilized life.)

Sidney turned his efforts to the Labour Party. He became its intellectual leader, finally entering Parliament, and Beatrice served on several government committees. The duo, like many political couples, became reluctant socialites, dining and hosting most of the great leaders of the time. Beatrice wrote, 'It is annoying not to be able to complete that big task of historical research to which we devoted so much time and money. But there seems to be a clear call to leadership in the Labour and Socialist Movement to which we feel that we must respond'.[55] Beatrice became increasingly jealous of Sidney's political career, fearing that he would eventually forget her and their work together. She wrote, 'Who knows how long I may have a large share of his life – how soon he may not belong body and soul to the nation?'[56]

In 1901, Beatrice was surprised by the sudden divorce of Chamberlain and his American wife. She longed for his companionship but resolved that her life was better spent working with Sidney. Her sexual frustrations with nine years of marriage to Sidney and her longing for Chamberlain brought a return of the psychosomatic depressive disorders of her youth. She obsessed over her own death, convinced that she was dying of a fatal illness, and was troubled by an acute case of eczema all over her body. Help came in the form of a doctor who practised alternative medicine and advised Beatrice to reduce her daily food intake to an absolute minimum. Eating a measured 16 ounces of food a day, Beatrice greatly reduced her weight to just over eight stone (112 lbs). This regimen seemed to give her the control over her body that she needed to refocus on her work. She wrote, 'Until I took to the rigid diet, the sensual side of my nature seemed to be growing at the expense of the intellectual'.[57] All of this, she hid from Sidney, and Sidney in turn did not notice. She continued this near-starvation diet until her death. That decision did not mean she regretted her 'partnership' with Sidney. Quite late in life she wrote, 'On the whole, then, I would advise the brain working woman to marry – if only she can find her Sidney'.[58]

Near the end of their long lives the Webbs slipped away from the social investigation of their youth and instead become advocates of the new British welfare state. Beatrice died in 1943 and Sidney in 1947. George Bernard Shaw arranged for them to be buried together in Westminster Abbey in December 1947.

Beatrice Webb rarely referred to herself as an economist. Her vision and talents were perhaps too broadly gauged to be so narrowly categorized. Still, her passion for the study of institutions connects her with a goodly company of other intellectuals, including Max Weber, Wesley C. Mitchell, John R. Commons and Thorstein Veblen, to mention just a few.

Notes

1. Webb, Beatrice (1891), *The Cooperative Movement in Great Britain*, 2nd edition 1899, London: Swan Sonnenschein, p. 2.
2. Webb, Beatrice (1926), *My Apprenticeship*, New York and London: Longmans, Green & Co, pp. 235, 247.
3. Seymour-Jones, Carole (1992), *Beatrice Webb: A Life*, Chicago: Ivan R. Dee, p. 6.
4. Seymour-Jones (1992), p. 6.
5. Radice, Lisanne (1984), *Beatrice and Sidney Webb: Fabian Socialists*, New York: St Martin's Press, p. 18.
6. Webb (1926), p. 18.
7. Radice (1984), p. 21.
8. Webb (1926), p. 45.
9. Radice (1984), p. 24.
10. Webb (1926), pp. 195–6.
11. Webb (1926), p. 165.
12. Radice (1984), p. 32.
13. Radice (1984), p. 33.
14. Webb (1926), p. 223.
15. Webb (1926), pp. 235, 247.
16. *Nineteenth Century*, (1887), **XXII**, pp. 483–99.
17. Webb (1926), p. 382.
18. Webb (1926), p. 334.
19. Webb, Beatrice (1948), *Our Partnership*, Barbara Drake and Margaret Cole (eds), New York and London: Longmans, Green & Co, p. 443.
20. Webb (1891), p. v.
21. Diary entry, 7 March 1889; in Webb, Beatrice (1982), *The Diary of Beatrice Webb*, N and J MacKenzie (eds), vol. 1, Cambridge, Mass.: Belknap Press.
22. Diary entry 2 July 1886, Webb, (1982), p. 173.
23. Diary entry 2 July 1886, Webb, (1982), p. 173.
24. Webb (1926), pp. 291–2,

25. Webb (1926), p. 440.
26. Webb (1926), p. 440.
27. Webb (1926), p. 445.
28. Webb (1926), p. 445.
29. Webb (1926), p. 392.
30. Diary entry, 15 February 1890, Webb (1982), p. 326.
31. Diary entry, 1 February 1890, Webb (1982), p. 322.
32. Diary entry, 13 February 1890, Webb (1982), p. 324.
33. Letter to B. Potter, 30 May 1890, Webb (1978), *The Letters of Sidney and Beatrice Webb*, N. Mackenzie (ed.), Cambridge: Cambridge University Press, pp. 141,143.
34. Letter to S. Webb, 23 August 1890, Webb (1978), pp. 178–9.
35. Letter to S. Webb, 8 August 1890, Webb (1978), pp. 201–2.
36. Letter to S. Webb, 4 December 1890, Webb (1978), p. 239.
37. Diary entry, 20 June 1891, Webb (1982), p. 357.
38. Radice (1984), p. 81.
39. Radice (1984), p. 84.
40. Diary entry for 23 July 1892; Webb (1982), p. 371.
41. Webb, Beatrice (1948), *Our Partnership*, Barbara Drake and Margaret Cole (eds), New York and London: Longmans, Green & Co., p. 87.
42. Webb, Sidney and Beatrice (1894) *The History of Trade Unionism*, revised edition 1920, London: Longmans, Green. Preface to original edition, p. xiii.
43. Webb (1948), p. 51.
44. Webb and Webb (1913), *Industrial Democracy*, Printed by the Authors for the Trade Unionists of the United Kingdom, p. 817.
45. Webb (1948), p. 174.
46. Webb (1948), p. 84.
47. Webb (1948), p. 195.
48. Webb (1948), p. 107.
49. Webb (1948), pp. 481–2.
50. Webb, Beatrice (1956), *Diaries, 1912–1924*, Margaret Cole (ed.), London and New York: Longmans, Green & Co., p. vii.
51. Webb (1948), p. 428.
52. Webb (1948), p. 435.
53. Webb (1948), p. 463.
54. Webb (1948), p. 464.
55. Webb (1956), p. 6.
56. Diary entry 1 December 1892; quoted in Radice (1984), p. 89.
57. Seymour-Jones (1992), p. 254.
58. Webb (1948), p. 46.

6 Joan Robinson (1903–83)

Born Joan Violet Maurice in 1903, she was always a 'bookish' girl. Her younger sister, with whom she shared a bedroom, remembered that Joan's lamp burned late into the night. She came early to delight in poetry and was observed to go to Hyde Park Corner once a week, where she read it aloud to those who cared to listen.[1] She rejected frivolity and paid little attention to appearance and attire. Instead, she took her studies very seriously and followed the emphasis that her family had always placed in knowledge and high moral principles. Her diligence in study led to her attendance at the very selective St Paul's School for Girls in London and later to Girton College, Cambridge.

Young women who attended Girton College were intellectual and privileged; as many maids served the students as there were students enrolled. Joan studied economics and recalled of her choice, 'I did not have much idea of what [economics] was about. I had some vague hope that it would help me to understand poverty and how it could be cured'.[2] Of her studies at Cambridge, she recalled:

> When I came up to Cambridge, in 1922, and started reading economics, Marshall's *Principles* was the Bible, and we knew little beyond it. Jevons, Cournot, even Ricardo, were figures in the footnotes. We heard of 'Pareto's Law', but nothing of the general equilibrium system. Sweden was represented by Cassel, America by Irving Fisher. Austria and Germany were scarcely known. Marshall was economics.[3]

Pigou delivered instruction in the Marshall tradition and Keynes gave a small number of exciting lectures on the actual problems on which he was working. Joan's work was excellent and her future as a teacher seemed promising. She developed the confidence and cleverness so necessary to a successful professor. While still a student, she and a woman colleague presented a satirical paper to the Marshall Society – an economist's tale of 'Beauty and the Beast' which some thought impertinent for an undergraduate. In the story, the merchant's daughter is to be wed to the beast, who turns into a handsome prince, and both experience great benefits in the transaction. He gains a considerable consumer's surplus by acquiring a beautiful wife and she a producer's surplus by engagement to a husband for whom she would have been willing to undergo irksome and unpleasant labour. The story concludes:

> With this happy union of producer's and consumer's surplus, they lived happily ever after, constantly keeping in mind their high ideals and maximizing their satisfaction by equalizing the marginal utility of each object of expenditure.[4]

All of Marshall's contrivances are present: elasticity, producer's and consumer's surpluses, maximizing of utility – the lot. Certainly the piece foreshadowed her disenchantment with Marshallian neoclassicism. It was probably unrelated that her results in the final examinations were not as high as she had hoped, a 'second' instead of the 'first' she desired.

While a student of Pigou, Joan's work had come to the attention of Austin Robinson. As a research fellow he was reading Pigou's papers and found hers 'quite exceptionally good'.[5] They struck up a friendship, and soon after she finished her degree they were married. The two sailed for India in 1926, where her husband was to tutor a young maharajah. Servants performed the ordinary household duties allowing Joan to study the economic world around her. This was her first exposure to the underdeveloped world and she was saddened by the poverty she observed. It was a subject to which she would return later in her career. She did some teaching in the local school and thus maintained contact with young students. She also became involved in the question of internal barriers to trade in India and participated in discussions on these issues with the foreign secretary even after her return to England in 1929.

Joan and Austin Robinson returned to Cambridge and found it alive with intellectual activity. Austin joined the Cambridge Faculty of Economics as a Lecturer. Joan did not have a formal position within the university, but she made herself available for tutoring and lectures. The Robinsons attended Keynes's lectures on the *Treatise on Money* in the autumn of 1930 and joined the 'Circus', a discussion group that included Richard Kahn, Piero Sraffa and James Meade. It was an exciting time for Joan, who was starting her family and her academic career at the same time. She received her first academic appointment as a university assistant lecturer in 1934. Promotions followed: university Lecturer in 1937, Reader in 1949, and Professor in 1965. She retired in 1971, but remained active in the profession.

Her first major work was *The Economics of Imperfect Competition*. It was written in the manner of Marshall, but went beyond Marshall in investigating cases that he had not covered. A preliminary finding that facilitated her analysis was that of the marginal revenue curve, an idea that emerged as a result of a luncheon of the Robinsons and their friend Richard Kahn. Austin Robinson was discussing the work of his student

Charles Gifford, who was exploring the idea. In fact, it appears that several scholars were investigating the concept at the same time. In the Forward to *The Economics of Imperfect Competition*, Robinson described the spontaneous process as follows:

> A moment has been reached in the development of economic theory when certain definite problems require to be solved, and many writers are at work upon them independently. There are many occasions, therefore, when several explorers are surprised, and somewhat pained, on meeting each other at the Pole. Of such an occasion the history of the 'marginal revenue curve' presents a striking example. This piece of apparatus plays a great part in my work, and my book arose out of the attempt to apply it to various problems, but I was not myself one of the many arrived in rapid succession at the Pole. . . . At this Pole I can claim to have arrived by a route of my own, but his [Harrod's] analytical formulation between average and marginal value has been of very great service to me since it appeared.[6]

In addition to the idea of the marginal revenue curve, Robinson responded to a 'pregnant' suggestion made by Piero Sraffa in an *Economic Journal* article. She wrote, 'It was Sraffa's view . . . that the whole theory of value should be treated in terms of monopoly analysis'.[7] From these two concepts *The Economics of Imperfect Competition* grew in the fertile ground of economic theory in Cambridge.

Until 1933 there was no understanding, and hence no systematic analysis, of market structures other than Marshall's perfect competition or pure monopoly. In the serious depression of the early thirties, the perfectly competitive model predicted that many firms would be forced to cease operations and close their doors. While this did occur to some extent, it was observed that a large number of firms seemed to be maximizing returns at restricted output levels. Nowhere in Marshall's system was an explanation to be found. The purpose of any theory is to explain as closely as possible conditions of the real world; but his theory was empty of content except for the polar cases. It was here that Robinson's contribution was made; she provided a statement of conditions of market equilibrium applicable to a whole range of market structures between perfect competition and pure monopoly – for all of the variations of *imperfect* competition.

Robinson recognized that the theory must be able to explain the *intermediate* cases. In the real world, firms do compete with each other, and they have some control over their market and the price they charge. There is often a purposeful differentiation of products, which introduces an element of monopoly. Each firm has a small monopoly of its own product. Furthermore, in industries where producers are large and few, firms behave differently than in those where there are many small, independent producers. The larger firms, known as oligopolies, restrict output; they charge higher prices and tend not to alter these prices; they make decisions with the expectation that other firms in the industry will react to their decisions and that they in turn must be alert to the decisions of others. In short, oligopolies are dependent on each other and they realize it. Hence, Robinson recognized that rather than a condition of independence of individual competitive firms in the marketplace, the normal case was one of interdependence.

As has happened more than a few times in the development of economics, more than one researcher, each unknown to the other, were exploring the same virgin territory and produced their conclusions at almost exactly the same time. The theory of imperfect competition was also being explored by Edward H. Chamberlin (1899–1967), who presented the results in a Harvard University dissertation, entitled *The Theory of Monopolistic Competition*, also published in 1933. At a much later date Professor Robinson referred to other equally fortuitous parallels in economics, writing, 'Such coincidences . . . are an indication that a stage has been reached in the evolution of a subject when there is a particular next step that has to be taken'.[8] Thus the two authors, Robinson and Chamberlin, share credit for their research in this area. Both started from the premise that aspects of monopoly were more typical than exceptional. Robinson concerned herself primarily with competition among the few, while Chamberlin concerned himself with monopoly among the many.

Robinson's book is not an easy one. It employs rigorous abstract analysis and detailed diagrams. She admits to readers that, 'the level of abstraction maintained in this book is distressingly high'.[9] With intricate diagrams, she provides a statement of conditions of market equilibrium applicable to the whole spectrum of market structures: from competition to all of the intermediate variations of 'imperfect' competition. This was a particularly important analysis because it led to two conclusions: 1) demand rather than marginal cost determined levels of output for firms, and 2) the 'cleansing' of the industry of inefficient firms, which some economists claimed happened during a downturn, simply didn't occur. Most could survive at output combinations of low quantity and high price.

Robinson stated that her main subject of investigation was value, but her study led her from the analysis of value into such topics as price discrimination, monopoly, monopsony,[10] marginal productivity, market exploitation, and the concept of the 'kinked' demand curve. She emphasized that, while the type of competition that characterizes oligopolies is different from the competition conceived by Adam Smith and other classical economists, the oligopolies' motivation for profits is no less strong, and the mechanism by which they make their decisions is quite similar to the analysis that had previously been applied to perfectly competitive conditions. 'Thus,' she wrote:

> the common-sense rule that the individual will equate marginal gains (whether of utility or marginal revenue) with marginal cost, applies to monopsony, to monopoly, and to perfect competition . . .. The cases which arise in perfect competition are only special cases of the general rule that the individual will equate marginal cost with marginal gain.[11]

Mrs Robinson's explanation of the price behaviour of oligopolies was made graphic by the so-called kinked demand curve, which shows that, if an oligopoly tries to raise prices, the volume of its sales will decline sharply as it loses customers to rival firms who do not follow its price increase; and if it lowers prices it does not gain new customers because competing firms will usually lower their prices as well. Hence oligopolies try to rid themselves of uncertainty by means of cartel and price-leadership agreements, and thus their prices become rigid and non-competitive. Oligopolies do compete in other ways, such as service and quality, but for them to compete in prices is impractical. In the author's words:

> . . . any conventional pattern of behaviour which establishes itself amongst an imperfectly competitive group provides a stable result. So long as all adhere to the same set of conventions each can enjoy his share of the market, and each can imagine that he is acting according to the strict rules of competition, although in fact the group as a whole, by unconscious collusion, are imposing a mild degree of monopoly upon the market.[12]

A further conclusion was one to which Robinson would return later: wages under perfect competition are normally less than the value of the marginal product of labour. Subsequently Professor Robinson observed that, while the work presented a static approach within the short-period aspect of competition, its strong points are negative. First, by showing that perfect competition cannot prevail in manufacturing industry, it demonstrates that price does not equal marginal cost and thereby undermines the traditional teaching orthodoxy that rests upon the assumptions of the perfectly competitive market. Second, it shows that consumer sovereignty can never prevail so long as market initiative, through the use of vast advertising and marketing budgets, lies with the producer. And third, it proves that with oligopolists in command of the market, wages are not equal to but are in fact considerably less than the value of the marginal product of labour, thus negating equity in the distribution of income. Each of these points generated arguments for the need of a new approach to economic theory, one that acknowledged that a new economic structure had replaced the assumptions on which the ideology of *laissez-faire* was based. Robinson's plea for a revision of economic theory based on realism was a thesis she emphasized over and over again.

Soon after the publication in January 1936 of *The General Theory of Employment, Interest and Money*, Joan Robinson established herself as an ardent disciple of Keynes and an eloquent interpreter of his work. *The General Theory* was destined to become an indestructible landmark in economic theory, but it was not meant to be Keynes's final work on this topic. Had his work not been cut short by his death in 1946, he would have extended his own work into areas not covered in *The General Theory.* Robinson was well placed to take on that work, having participated in discussions at the Circus on the evolution of Keynes's thinking from the time of his *Treatise on Money* published in 1930.

Robinson's *Introduction to the Theory of Employment*, appearing in 1937, provided one of the first explanations of elements of Keynes's analysis as it dealt with the topics of investment and saving, the multiplier, employment and unemployment, prices and the rate of interest.[13] In the same year appeared her *Essays in the Theory of Employment* in which she used Keynesian theory to interpret several particular problems and found application of Keynes's work to additional areas. In 13 essays, she applied the full extent of her analytical skills to examine such topics as full employment, mobility of labour, causes and remedies for unemployment, disinvestment, and the concept of zero saving. She recognized that Keynes's *General Theory* had been concerned chiefly with short-run analysis and she extended his work in an essay entitled 'The long-period theory of employment'. In highly abstract terms she set out 'to outline a method by which Mr Keynes's system of analysis may be extended into the regions of the long period and by which it may become possible to examine the long-period influences which are at work at any moment of time'.[14]

The final paper in *Essays in the Theory of Employment*, entitled 'Some reflections on Marxist economics', is a thorough inquiry of the untenable position in which a person finds himself, 'who simultaneously espouses Marxism and Say's Law, the one developing a theory to explain unemployment, while the other assumed that unemployment cannot exist'. It is a natural transition from this essay to *An Essay on Marxian Economics*, published in 1942, in which Robinson applied modern academic methods of analysis to Marxism. Concerned as she was with the future course of economic theory, she sought, by revealing the harmonies and conflicts between Marxism and academic economics, to discover a basis for their synthesis. First she traced the essentials of Marxian doctrine, and then she interpreted the 'mysticism' of his specialized vocabulary in terms of what she understood Marx to have been saying 'in language that an academic could understand'.[15] 'The substance of Marx's argument,' she remarked, 'is far from being irrelevant to the modern situation, but the argument has become incompatible with its verbal integument'.[16] On the other hand, she observed 'that some parts of the academic analysis can be separated from its unacceptable ideology and applied to real problems'.[17] She saw that Marx had flashes of unique understanding, although he was capable of making mistakes. She confirmed this opinion at a later date when she wrote:

> For a discussion of the questions nowadays found to be interesting – growth and stagnation, technical progress and the demand for labor, the balance of sectors in an expanding economy – Marxian theory provides a starting point where academic teaching was totally blank .... Marx, as a scientist, proclaimed this grand program, and made an impressive start upon it. But it got very little further. A school of thought flourishes when the followers continuously revise and sift the ideas of the founder, test his hypotheses, correct his errors, reconcile contradictions in his conclusions, and adapt his method to deal with fresh matter. It takes a great genius to set a new subject going; the disciples must admire, even reverence, the master, but they should not defer to him. On the contrary, they must be his closest critics.[18]

While Robinson noted in the 1942 essay 'that no point of substance in Marx's argument depends on the labor theory of value', she also pointed out that Marx implemented his bitter hatred of oppression by using terminology that 'derives its force from the moral indignation with which it is saturated'.[19]

Again Marx's search for a theory of causation of economic crises and his analysis of the balance between capital goods and consumption goods industries foreshadows Keynes's theory of employment. Here Robinson recognized the importance of long period analysis and, concluding on this note, she wrote:

> The theory of short period fluctuations in effective demand, opened up by Mr Keynes's *General Theory*, has already made great progress. Marx was mainly concerned with long run dynamic analysis, and this field is still largely untilled . . . Marx, however imperfectly he worked out the details, set himself the task of discovering the law of motion of capitalism, and if there is any

> hope of progress in economics at all, it must be in using academic methods to solve the problems posed by Marx.[20]

To this challenge Robinson herself responded in her next major treatise.

The topic of the accumulation of capital has been one of central concern to economists from Adam Smith to the present because the subject is basic to any examination of economic growth and development. Book II of Adam Smith's *The Wealth of Nations*, and Chapter 3 of Book II, were both entitled, 'The Accumulation of Capital'. Smith viewed capital accumulation, the division of labour and a widening market as the chief sources of economic growth. Rosa Luxemburg acknowledged the importance of the topic to Marxism when she wrote her major economic work, *The Accumulation of Capital* on the subject. Robinson wrote a penetrating interpretation and critique of Rosa Luxemburg's book in 1951, which appeared as an introduction to the English translation.

In 1956 Robinson produced a comprehensive work under the same title, a work that requires the best analytical equipment and diligence the reader can bring to it. *The Accumulation of Capital* discusses the dynamic long-run consequences of the accumulation of capital that investment in the short run brings about. Here the interplay of capital accumulation and technical progress is analysed in relation to the rate of growth and the rate of profit. It was found that the success of capitalism depends on technical progress, which may take the form of increases in productivity. This, in turn, requires capital accumulation at an appropriate rate.

The author began by defining the familiar concepts and categories required for the analysis of investment: income, wealth, capital, money and purchasing power. She found their meanings 'elusive', 'not very precise', 'paradoxical', 'metaphysical', but nonetheless 'useful'. For purposes of her own analysis she dissected the term 'equilibrium' (a concept she deemed treacherous), and introduced several new terms that reappear in several of her later writings:

> a state of *tranquility*: When an economy develops in a smooth, regular manner without internal contradictions or external shocks, so that expectations based upon past experience are very confidently held, and are in fact, constantly fulfilled and therefore renewed as time goes by.
>
> a condition of *lucidity*: when everyone is fully aware of the situation in all markets, and understands the technical properties of all commodities, both their use in production and the satisfaction that they give in consumption.
>
> a condition of *harmony* when the rules of the game are fully understood and accepted by everyone, in which no one tries to alter his share in the

> proceeds of the economy, and all combine to increase the total to be shared.[21]

The author acknowledged that:

> . . . it is only necessary to describe these conditions to see how remote they are from the states in which actual economies dwell. Capitalism, in particular, could never have come into existence in such conditions, for the divorce between work and property, which makes large-scale enterprise possible, entails conflict; and the rules of the game have been developed precisely to make accumulation and technical progress possible in conditions of uncertainty and imperfect knowledge. Yet, too much disturbance, deception and conflict would break an economy to pieces. The persistence of capitalism till to-day is evidence that certain principles of coherence are imbedded in its 'confusion'.[22]

Thereafter, in order to examine accumulation in the long run and to discover those 'certain principles of coherence', she built a succession of carefully controlled models, progressing from one based on highly simplified assumptions to others of increasing complexity, with 'the whole argument . . . set out, as far as possible, as an analytical construction, with a minimum of controversy'.[23]

In order to identify the conditions necessary for harmonious development Robinson introduced the concept of *a golden age*, a condition of neutral technical progress, which she acknowledges to be 'a mythical state of affairs not likely to obtain in any economy'.[24] It occurs, she wrote:

> when technical progress is neutral, and proceeding steadily without any change in the time pattern of production, the competitive mechanism working freely, population growing . . . at a steady rate and accumulation going on fast enough to supply productive capacity for all available labour. [Then] the rate of profit tends to be constant and the level of real wages to rise with output per man. There are then no internal contradictions in the system.[25]

Neutral technical progress occurs when the technical progress incorporated in new capital equipment is neither capital-using nor capital-saving. While it does not alter the capital/labour ratios in the economy, it increases the productivity of labour uniformly in the entire economy. With capital accumulation progressing at a steady rate and with no political disturbances, the system develops smoothly. 'Total annual output and the stock of capital (valued in terms of commodities) then grow together at a constant proportionate rate compounded of the rate of increase of the labour force and the rate of increase of output per man'.[26] In a series of interim conclusions, she found that 'The rate of technical progress and the rate of increase of the labour force . . . govern the rate of growth of output of an economy that can be permanently maintained at a constant rate of profit'.[27] Thus, 'When the potential growth rate is being realized the economy is in a golden age'.[28]

The book continues in its 435 pages and 36 chapters with intricate discussions of prices, wages, investment, and profits in the short run, and with separate sections dealing with finance, land, and international trade – the whole a *tour de force* of precision thinking by means of deductive analysis. Robinson's analytical work on the importance of technical progress to economic development, is notable since good empirical studies on the relative importance of increased capital per worker and technical progress were not published until the period 1962–1966, some six years later.

Utilizing some of the concepts in *The Accumulation of Capital*, Robinson turned from writing for members of the economics profession to writing for students, *Exercises in Economic Analysis*, which appeared in 1961. Much of the analysis of the earlier work, with its specialized vocabulary and its methodology of model building, reappears here. In the *Exercises* the author produced a unique textbook that demonstrates without definitions or diagrams how the principles of economic science can be developed from tightly knit reasoning and rational constructs. Without attempting to explain analytical method, she demonstrates it. Instead of supplying graphs, she gives instructions to the reader on how to construct them, so that the reader can see not only their derivation but also the value of using graphical analytical techniques. This work was not intended to be an exhaustive treatise like most introductory texts, yet it covers a broad range of both macroeconomics and microeconomics. Robinson stated that she tried merely to show the reader 'how propositions in economic theory are arrived at so that he can carry on for himself where the book leaves off'.[29]

In her next major work Robinson again emphasized the need for dynamic analysis in economic theory. Acknowledging that *The Accumulation of Capital* had been 'found excessively difficult' and oppressed by the awareness that 'accepted teaching was still doped by static equilibrium analysis' Robinson produced *Essays in the Theory of Economic Growth* in 1963. Here, determined 'to get economic analysis off the mud of static equilibrium theory', she developed her theme that economic analysis must be dynamic.[30]

The concept of equilibrium, a taken-for-granted tool in economics, was the critical focus of her attention. In relation to this analysis, she asked: 'What meaning can we attach to the conception of a position which is never reached at any particular moment in time, but which exists only in virtue of the fact that the parties concerned believe . . . that it will be reached in the future?'[31]

She answered her own question in *Economic Philosophy* with some sarcasm:

> Logical structures of this kind have a certain charm. They allow those without mathematics to catch a hint of what intellectual beauty means. This has been a great support to them in their ideological function. In the face of such elegance, only a philistine could complain that the contemplation of an ultimate stationary state, when accumulation has come to an end, is not going to help us very much with the problems of today.[32]

She also commented:

> The concept of equilibrium, of course, is an indispensable tool of analysis. . . . But to use the equilibrium concept one has to keep it in its place, and its place is strictly in the preliminary states of an analytical argument, not in the framing of hypotheses to be tested against the facts, for we know perfectly well that we shall not find facts in a state of equlibrium.[33]

Robinson then moved from her analysis of equilibrium in static microeconomic analysis to an analysis of the concept of general equilibrium in classical, neoclassical and Keynesian models.

In relation to general equilibrium in microeconomic analysis, traditional economics has long taught that 'At any moment there is a certain equilibrium position towards which the system is tending, but the position of equilibrium shifts faster than the system can move towards any one position of equilibrium'.[34] Robinson promptly went beyond this, and observed, 'An economy may be in equilibrium from a short-period point of view and yet contain within itself incompatibilities that are soon going to knock it out of equilibrium'.[35] She reasoned that 'No one would deny that to speak of a tendency towards equilibrium – that itself shifts the position towards which it is tending – is a contradiction in terms'.[36]

Thereafter the concept of equilibrium in her analysis became a dynamic concept, influenced by seven independent determinants that are established by the rules and motives governing human behaviour in the economy under examination. For a free economy, these determinants are: technical conditions, investment policy; thriftiness conditions, competitive conditions, the wage bargain, financial conditions and the initial stock of capital goods and the state of expectations formed by past experience. When these determinants combine in a fortuitous manner to achieve smooth, steady growth with full employment, 'a golden age', that state of mythical equilibrium, results. The unlikelihood of this occurring in a free market is obvious, as Robinson pointed out:

> To set out the characteristics of a golden age by no means implies a prediction that it is likely to be realized in any actual period of history. The concept is useful, rather, as a means of distinguishing various types of disharmony that are liable to arise in an uncontrolled economy.[37]

Subsequently, in a succession of models using highly abstract analysis, she demonstrated how each of the several determinants of equilibrium affects the level of operation in the economy. In 'A neo-neoclassical theorem' the author arrived at the following proposition:

> When the conception of the rate of profit determined by the rate of accumulation of capital and thriftiness conditions is combined with the conception of a choice of technique from a given spectrum of possibilities, it can be seen that the highest rate of output of consumption goods is achieved when the rate of profit on capital is equal to the rate of accumulation.[38]

Later she simplified this to state that general equilibrium could be achieved when 'the rate of profit on capital is equal to the rate of growth of the economy' but she observed that actual conditions are far from realizing this balance.[39] She cautioned that it was not legitimate to draw practical conclusions from such highly abstract and theoretical explorations as had been conducted, but she could not refrain from observing that 'if there is any rough correspondence between reality and the type of analysis here set out, the fact that the rate of profit on capital may be of the order of 15 or 20 per cent in any economy that is growing at the rate of 2 or 3 per cent per annum, does suggest some interesting lines of thought'.[40]

Continuing her criticism of academic economists, Robinson then addressed Lionel Robbins's argument that economic science should be value free. Proponents of this view believed that economists should not choose goals but only describe various paths to attain goals chosen by others. Robinson responded, writing that, 'it is not possible to describe [an economic] *system* without moral judgements creeping in' and 'because the subject is necessarily soaked in moral feelings, judgement is coloured by prejudice'.[41]

Robinson then asked the obvious questions: does economic growth matter after all? Why should we care? Later, she answers the question in the manner of John Stuart Mill:

> . . . growth for its own sake is not a rational objective of policy. It would be

> a rational use of growing resources to remove poverty, to clear up the hideous legacy of the industrial revolution, to build the schools and hospitals and train the personnel that the social services urgently require, as well as to modernize industry. It would be necessary to carry out technical and social research to see what needs to be done. The rate of return in benefit to society of investment would certainly be shown to be very high, so that a policy would require growth for a long time to come. Growth should be the consequence, not the aim, of rational economic policy.[42]

Realistically, Robinson found the choices for the future that must be made, whether on behalf of world policy, national policy, or the internal operation of the economy. The answers must be sought within ideological frameworks that are complex and often contradictory. In a world where 'a genuinely unversalist point of view is very rare', international problems must be resolved within the compass of nationalism.[43] National policy, on the other hand, is formulated largely within a *laissez-faire* ideology. Its bias dominates our thinking when we seek solutions, for example, to the problem of poverty amidst plenty, or to the problems of what is a well balanced pattern of private and public investment. Nor do we have a clear philosophy to guide individual decision makers in an industrial economy as they flounder in confusion between those courses of action that yield the greatest profit and those that yield the greatest social benefit. To these matters Robinson found no easy solutions. Dealing with them in her final chapter of *Economic Philosophy*, 'What are the rules of the game?', she concluded:

> The moral problem is a conflict that can never be settled. Social life will always present mankind with a choice of evils. No metaphysical solution that can ever be formulated will seem satisfactory for long. The solutions offered by economists were no less delusory than those of the theologians that they displaced.[44]

Applied economics claimed her attention in her next book, *Economics: An Awkward Corner*, published in 1967. Here she abandoned the impersonality of the rigid abstract analysis that dominated her previous studies and concerned herself with contemporary policy. In a series of six short essays on income and prices; the balance of trade; international finance; employment and growth; monopoly and competition; and work and property, she reveals her social philosophy as that of a modern humanist as she discusses, with particular reference to Great Britain, the current status of these several issues and finds the British economy at 'an awkward phase in the continuing process of historical development'.[45]

Many of her observations were as applicable to the economy of the

United States as to that of Great Britain. In both societies ideological contradictions abound. The ideology of *laissez-faire* survives in spite of the evident need for government planning to maintain employment goals, satisfactory levels of money incomes and prices, and a balance of international payments. Modern society, with its large productive capacity, and potential for less social inequality, avoids greater equality of income distribution because we have 'no philosophy to guide us in sharing it out'.[46]

Such are the contradictions, Robinson thought, of modern capitalism; she wrote, they 'arise from the need to readjust the organization of Society to the fantastic capacity for production of material wealth that the application of science to technology has made possible'.[47] Economics can point the way, but it cannot impose the correctives. 'The obstacles to such schemes are neither technical nor legal. They lie in the political opposition that could be rallied against them at home and the threat of flights of capital and capitalists to more congenial shores'.[48] Truly, she wrote, economics is in 'an awkward corner'. 'Perhaps in the end', Robinson concluded, 'the facts of life, like a sheepdog with an awkward flock, will finally nudge democracy towards common sense'.[49]

Three years later Robinson continued this theme but used a different approach in *Freedom and Necessity, An Introduction to the Study of Society*, a panoramic view of the role of economics in human history. It was compact (124 pages), wide ranging and a brilliant social history of economic science. As an economic anthropologist, Robinson searches in the early chapters for the reasons for species survival and examines the ways by which various species have developed skills needed for survival, for learning correct social behaviour and for establishing a hierarchy of ranks. There follows, in the tradition of nineteenth century philosophical radicals, a search for origins: the concept of private property, the organization of warfare, the economics of capital accumulation and investment, the rationalization of race and social class, and notions of democracy and national patriotism. The interplay of freedom and necessity 'which is the characteristic of human life', was found to express itself in many ways in the course of societal evolution, as we have endeavoured to resolve the endless conflict between the freedom of the individual and the necessity of the group.

The author observes that 'there are three characteristics of the modern age which distinguish us from the past – the hypertrophy of the nation state . . . the application of science to production and the penetration of money values into every aspect of life'.[50] She continues:

> Scientific discoveries were still often made in the pursuit of knowledge for

its own sake, but the profit motive provided digestive organs that absorbed them into productive technology. The spiral action of technical development was set going which has been spinning ever since at a more and more vertiginous rate.[51]

Thereafter, in brilliant vignettes she identified successive views of social progress as held by, among others, Ricardo, Marx, and Marshall – the latter's 'vision of industry at the service of mankind' having been distorted into a 'nightmare of terror' by modern militarism and war.[52] In the course of exploring the contemporary scene, she writes '. . . the profit motive contains no mechanism to ensure that technical progress will take digestible forms. . . . Modern capitalism is well adapted to produce fabulous technical successes but not to provide the bases for the noble life accessible to all that Marshall dreamed of'.[53] She continues incisively:

> The requirements of the warfare state and the welfare state meet in the export of armaments, which keep industry in ex-imperialist countries prosperous and permits enmities in the ex-colonial countries, which were frozen at the level of bows and arrows or flintlocks, to break out with bombs and tanks.[54]

After examining how some modern economies – Sweden, Soviet Russia, Maoist China, and new nations of the Third World – have organized themselves, Robinson remarks that the time has come when we should advance into a new state of social self-conciousness beyond *laissez-faire* profit motivation. She writes:

> The task of social science now is to raise self-consciousness to the second degree, to find out the causes, the mode of functioning and the consequences of the adoption of ideologies, so as to submit them to rational criticism. Only too often would-be scientists are still operating at the first degree, propagating some ideology which serves some particular interest, as the economists' doctrine of laissez-faire served the interest of capitalist business.[55]

Values, she believes, should be searched for openly and judged on their own merits, rather than letting:

> commercial considerations swallow up more and more of social life. So much so that those who want to demand, say, improvements in the health service find it politic to point to a loss of production due to sickness and those who are concerned with education evaluate its benefits in terms of the salaries of trained personnel.[56]

In two brilliant terminal chapters, 'False prophets' and 'Science and morality', Robinson chides her fellow professionals for failing to take a role of moral leadership: 'the function of social science is quite different from that of the natural sciences – that is, a conception of what is the proper way to behave and the permissible pattern of relationships in family, economic and political life'.[57] She returns to an argument made earlier in her career, the question of value judgements in the social sciences. She thinks it obvious that every human being has ideological, moral and political views. To pretend to have none, to be *purely objective* must necessarily be either self-deception or a device to deceive others. She continues, 'To eliminate value judgments from the subject matter of social science is to eliminate the subject itself, for since it concerns human behaviour it must be concerned with the value judgments that people make'.[58]

Freedom and necessity today, according to Professor Robinson, require an ideology that rests on a moral philosophy that defines an accepted code of social behaviour and involves more than the freedom to make money. On this note she challenges both her students and fellow social scientists as she concludes:

> The economics of the laissez-faire school purported to abolish the moral problem by showing that the pursuit of self interest by each individual rebounds to the benefit of all. The task of the generation now in rebellion is to reassert the authority of morality over technology; the business of social scientists is to help them to see both how necessary and how difficult that task is going to be.[59]

Economic Heresies, appearing in 1971, is a brilliant sequel to *Freedom and Necessity*, directed to a different audience. Whereas the latter dealt provocatively with topics of broad popular interest, *Economic Heresies* is an ingeniously original review of the development of economic thought. It is an economist's gold mine. In it, as indicated by its subtitle, 'Some old-fashioned questions in economic theory', Robinson goads her fellow economists to revise the theoretical structures of economics to fit the realities with which they purport to deal. It is as though she is responding to the challenge that Beatrice Webb issued in 1906 to sweep away the fallacies in the subject of economics. It is not any easy task. Robinson's own words, written in the context of appraising a respected colleague's work, are equally appropriate to her own work:

> It is no wonder that this book took a long time to write. It will not be read quickly. Addicts of pure economic logic who find their craving ill satisfied by the wishy-washy products peddled in contemporary journals have here a double-distilled elixir that they can enjoy, drop by drop, for many a day.[60]

Beginning with the observation that classical economic theory was founded on a set of hypothetical assumptions that supported *laissez-faire*, free trade, the gold standard, and the profit system in a competitive free market – conditions that have long since ceased to prevail in reality – Robinson notes that Keynes's efforts to look at the actual situation in a functioning economy backfired as his views became orthodox. 'Keynes', she wrote:

> was looking at the actual situation and trying to understand how an actual economy operates; he brought the argument down from timeless stationary states into the present, here and now, when the past cannot be changed and the future cannot be known. At the time it seemed like a revolution. . . . After 1945, Keynes's innovations had become orthodox in their turn; now governments had to admit that they were concerned with maintaining the level of employment; but in respect to economic theory the old theology closed in again. . . . But once Keynes has become orthodox, the case is altered. If we are to be guaranteed near full employment the question comes up, what form should employment take? . . . The complacency of neo-laissez faire cuts the economists off from discussing the economic problems of today just as Say's Law cut them off from discussing unemployment in the world slump.[61]

Thereafter, she subjects to reexamination the assumptions of each of the favourite economic models – Walras, Wicksell, Marshall, Pigou, Keynes, Harrod – and the origins of familiar economic doctrines. She examines increasing and diminishing returns, the quantity theory of money, the theory of the firm, effective demand and growth analysis; she finds each, in its orthodox treatment, deficient by reason of its inability to provide an interpretation of present reality. She notes, for example, Keynes's failure to distinguish between profitable investment and socially beneficial investment, writing:

> Avoiding slumps is all to the good as far as it goes, but now there is growing up, especially in the United States, a protest against the wasteful or pernicious lines of production into which government and industry direct resources, and their failure to provide for the basic human needs of the population. The neo-neoclassical economists cannot take any part in this great debate as long as they have nothing to contribute to it except the tattered remnants of the laissez-faire doctrine that what is profitable is right.[62]

Again, after a provocative discussion of the irreversibility of technical change, she observes:

> Economists have not much emphasized the opposite kind of irreversibility – the destruction of resources, the devastation of amenities, and the accumu-

> lation of poison in air and water. Pigou made a great point of 'external diseconomies' such as the smoke nuisance, but, within the confines of his stationary state, he could not emphasize *permanent* losses. It has been left rather to the natural scientists to sound the alarm, while orthodox economists, unperturbed, continue to elaborate the presumption in favor of laissez-faire.[63]

She concludes, 'It is easy enough to make models on stated assumptions. The difficulty is to find the assumptions that are relevant to reality.... A model that is intended to be relevant to some actual problem must take account of the mode of operation of the economy to which it refers'.[64] Instead of being content to be impeded by an outmoded theoretical scheme, she urges economists to begin again with Keynes's assumptions (a private enterprise economy facing an uncertain future, in which investment and employment decisions are made by firms in an imperfectly competitive market) and devise a model appropriate to today's capitalist industrialized nations that seek their modern goals in a setting markedly different from the setting for which Keynes wrote. She adds:

> ... modern capitalism for the last twenty-five years has been closely bound up with the armaments race and the trade in weapons (not to mention wars when they are used); it has not succeeded in helping ... to promote development in the Third World. Now we are told that it is in the course of making the planet uninhabitable even in peacetime. It should be the duty of economists to do their best to enlighten the public about the economic aspects of these menacing problems.[65]

Robinson returned to the theme of *Economic Heresies* in her lecture 'The second crisis of economic theory' delivered at the annual meeting of the American Economic Association in December 1971. The Richard T. Ely lecture gave Professor Robinson the opportunity to present to the mostly American audience what she saw as the two crises in economic theory in her lifetime. Both, she thought, were errors of omission based on the failure of economic theory to take on real world problems. The first crisis arose out of the great depression of the 1930s: the failure of the profession to understand the causes of mass unemployment and to offer reasonable programmes to bring it to an end. The second crisis arose out of the first: the failure of the profession during the post-World War II decades to address the purpose of full employment and growth. Granted that full employment was desirable, how were the benefits to be distributed among the world's people? She challenged the profession by adding, 'We have not got a theory of distribution. We have nothing to say on the subject which above all others occupies the minds of people who economics is supposed to enlighten'.[66] Many who heard her or read her address later thought that she stood that night at the peak of her powers.

In the last decade of her life, Robinson continued to address the unanswered questions. Like many of the rest of us, she thought she knew less about the world near the end of her career than at the beginning. Yet she continued to ask the questions that it would have been more comfortable to ignore. Most frequently these questions arose in two related areas of economic science: distribution and methodology.

At a time when economic growth seemed to be the passion of practitioners, she asked its purpose. Is any growth better than none? Do we want to press for full employment when the output may intensify the arms race and lower the quality of some people's lives? Do we want full employment when it increases the disparity between rich and poor? Do we want full employment and growth if the accompanying externalities foul the very earth on which we live? Why don't we have answers to these questions by now; are we not a moral science? Or, do we just not care? At the age of 75 Robinson commented, 'We [economists] are sitting around discussing ideas totally beside the point. The important question is . . . whether our generation will succeed in destroying the world . . . Economists should begin to address the important issue of our impending doom'.[67]

Indeed she wrote as if economics had lost its roots in moral philosophy – in the larger questions of Smith and Mill. Were we so caught up in pursuing each minor destination that we failed to consider our direction? Robinson thought we were. She claimed that the economics profession had drifted away from the fundamental questions. She accused us of abandoning the mission to analyse the real world, of attaching ourselves to fairy tales. It was still the 'disintegration of economics' she queried in the 1950s. In fact, she believed that there is no such thing as a *purely* economic problem and we have shielded ourselves from this fact by assuming away the interesting and important questions. We have turned our backs on the challenges so obvious in the Third World.

When Wesley Clair Mitchell wrote that a great economist was one who tackled the biggest issues, he might well have been talking about Robinson's work. In fact, it is likely that there are few current economists who would not recognize that she addressed the most difficult questions, even if they did not agree with her answers. She raised the issue of morality in the economic world when others didn't. That she didn't have all of the answers does not detract from her legacy. Indeed, she would have been happy to have been described as 'a destroyer of myths, a clearer of ground upon which someone else will build'.[68] She rang the bell to attract the attention of her fellow economists to the important questions, and she relished doing so over an outstanding career of 50 years.

Notes

1. Letter of Phyllis Maurice to Marjorie Turner, postmarked 14 January, 1988. Quoted in Marjorie S. Turner, (1989), *Joan Robinson and the Americans*, London: M.E. Sharp, p. 10.
2. Statement of Joan Robinson, quoted from Turner (1989), p. 17.
3. Quoted from Turner (1989), p. 17.
4. Robinson, Joan and Dorothea Morison (1966), 'Beauty and the Beast', in *Collected Economic Papers*, Vol. 1, Oxford; Basil Blackwell, pp. 225–33.
5. Turner (1989), p. 16.
6. Robinson, Joan (1964a), *The Economics of Imperfect Competition*, London: Macmillan & Co., first published 1933, Forword, p. xiv.
7. Robinson, (1964a), Forword, p. xiii.
8. Robinson, Joan (1962a), *Economic Philosophy*, Chicago: Aldine Publishing Co., p. 104.
9. Robinson, Joan (1962a), p. 327.
10. Robinson invented the word 'monopsony' to mean 'single buyer'.
11. Robinson, (1962a), p. 230.
12. Robinson, Joan (1964b), *An Essay on Marxian Economics*, London: Macmillan & Co., p. 78.
13. Robinson, Joan (1969), *Introduction to the Theory of Employment*, first published 1937, London: Macmillan & Co.
14. Robinson, Joan (1953), *Essays in the Theory of Employment*, first published 1937, Oxford: Basil Blackwell, p. 75.
15. Robinson, Joan (1966), *An Essay on Marxian Economics*, first published 1942, London, Macmillan & Co., p. vii.
16. Robinson (1966), p. 19.
17. Robinson (1966), p. v.
18. Robinson, Joan (1962b), 'Marxism: Religion and Science', *Monthly Review*, December, pp. 424, 434.
19. Robinson (1966), p. 22.
20. Robinson (1966), p. 95.
21. Robinson, Joan (1965), *The Accumulation of Capital*, first published 1956, London: Macmillan & Co., p. 59.
22. Robinson (1965), p. 60.
23. Robinson (1965), Preface, p. x.
24. Robinson (1965), p. 99.
25. Robinson (1965), p. 99.
26. Robinson (1965), p. 99.
27. Robinson (1965), p. 173.
28. Robinson (1965), p. 173.
29. Robinson, Joan (1961), *Exercises in Economic Analysis*, London: Macmillan & Co., p. 5.
30. Robinson, Joan (1963), *Essays in the Theory of Economic Growth*, London: Macmillan & Co., Preface, p. v.
31. Robinson (1963), p. 23.
32. Robinson (1962a), p. 61.
33. Robinson (1962a), p. 81.
34. Robinson (1966), p. 59.
35. Robinson (1963), p. 26.
36. Robinson (1962a), p. 83.

37. Robinson (1963), pp. 98–9.
38. Robinson (1963), p. 120.
39. Robinson (1963), p. 132.
40. Robinson (1963), p. 132.
41. Robinson (1962a), pp. 14, 23.
42. Robinson, Joan (1967), *Economics: An Awkward Corner*, New York: Pantheon Books, p. 43.
43. Robinson, Joan (1962a), p. 126.
44. Robinson (1962a), p. 146.
45. Robinson (1967), p. 3.
46. Robinson (1967), p. 5.
47. Robinson (1967), p. 6.
48. Robinson (1967), p. 62.
49. Robinson (1967), p. 83.
50. Robinson, Joan (1970), *Freedom and Necessity*, London: George Allen & Unwin, p. 60.
51. Robinson (1970), p. 63.
52. Robinson (1970), p. 71.
53. Robinson (1970), p. 87.
54. Robinson (1970), p. 93.
55. Robinson (1970), p. 122.
56. Robinson (1970), p. 118.
57. Robinson (1970), p. 120.
58. Robinson (1970), p. 122.
59. Robinson (1970), p. 124.
60. Sraffa, Piero, in Robinson, *Collected Economic Papers*, vol. 3, (1965) Oxford: Basil Blackwell, p. 7.
61. Robinson, Joan (1971), *Economic Heresies, Some Old-Fashioned Questions in Economic Theory*, New York: Basic Books, pp. xv, xx, xxi.
62. Robinson (1971), p. 50–51.
63. Robinson (1971), p. 55.
64. Robinson (1971), pp. 141, 142.
65. Robinson (1971), pp. 143–4.
66. Robinson, Joan, (1972), 'The Second Crisis of Economic Theory', *The American Economic Review*: Papers and Proceedings of the Eighty-fourth Annual Meeting of the American Economic Association, New Orleans, Louisiana, December 27–29, 1971, **LXII**, 2, May pp. 1–10.
67. Robinson, Joan, (1983), *Monthly Review*, October 1983, pp. 15–17.
68. Arrow, Kenneth. Quoted from Turner, (1989), p. 213.

7 Irma Adelman (1930—)

Irma Adelman, like many economists before and after, chose the profession because she wanted to help people to have longer and happier lives. This goal might seem to apply more closely to a medical practitioner, but many economists, including Alfred Marshall, have expressed the same ambition. She believed, 'My perception at the time was that economic problems were the most important problems that humanity had to face'.[1] Specifically, she was interested in how persistent poverty could be alleviated.

Adelman was born before the outbreak of World War II in Romania. Her father had fled Russia after the revolution and had become a successful socialist businessman. Her mother had been a student of Joseph Schumpeter when he taught at the University of Cernowitz. Her parents were Jewish and placed a high value on education. They sent their only child to a French Catholic nuns' school which they considered the best education available and she did not disappoint her parents. Irma was encouraged in her studies by her mother, who hoped her daughter would have the successful career she had been denied by circumstances in Romania. Recognizing the signs of danger for Jews, Adelman's father had the foresight to leave Romania in 1939 and moved the family to Palestine. There she finished her pre-univeristy programme with high marks and fought in the Israeli war of independence.

Adelman left Israel to further her education and enrolled in 1949 as an undergraduate at the University of California, Berkeley. She opted for the study of business and public administration and shifted to economics as a graduate student. In what must have been record time, she emerged with a PhD just six years after entering the university. Originally, she had planned to return to Israel to assume whatever duties would best serve the new state. Instead, she met and married her husband, Frank Adelman, a graduate student in physics. With some guilt about planning her future in the United States, she pursued her goal of helping the world's people by utilizing her knowledge of economic processes.

Adelman thought her graduate education was incomplete because the Department of Economics at Berkeley provided minimal preparation in mathematics. She had studied with Robert Dorfman and learned econometrics from George Kuznets. She added to her knowledge by enrolling in courses offered by the mathematics, statistics and agricultural economics departments.

Methodology issues also interested her, even at this early stage of her career. She benefited particularly from discussion of the scientific method with her husband, who explained an approach used by applied physicists. The technique made use of a continual iterative process between theory and experimental or statistical 'facts'. Facts led to refined theories and theories to new research; it was a two-way process, a double feedback between theory and statistical findings. This iterative method allowed her to keep the real world of observed data as a constant reference and led to one of the strongest elements of her future work – the search for real world data on which to base her work, a major omission of many of her contemporaries.

Her early research was well received and she looked forward to a successful academic career. Unfortunately, it was not to be that easy. Even though she had graduated at the top of her class from a prestigious university, she was unable to get a tenure-track appointment. She became what is now known as a 'freeway flier', an academic who works at one or more universities, travels substantial distances and hopes for a regular position. Her frustration with one-year appointments continued at Berkeley, Mills College and Stanford University. Yet, somehow she was able to publish eight articles in major economic and statistical journals and one book, *Theories of Economic Growth and Development*.[2]

One of the articles written during this difficult period has since been identified as a 'classic', one of the best 20 articles ever published in *Econometrica*.[3] The paper confirmed the Frisch hypothesis of the random origin of business cycles and involved the use of a computer even before the days of Fortran. Of the birth of the article, Adelman wrote:

> The Klein–Goldberger paper arose when my husband, a physicist, one day expressed a desire to try programming a simple problem and asked whether there was anything in economics that might be suitable. I suggested the Klein–Goldberger model. This was in 1955, before the days of Fortran; all programming was in machine language. I remember spreading out a large sheet of paper on the floor, with a map of the computer memory, and keeping track of the location of individual variables after every operation. Nevertheless, when we ran the problem there was only one error in the code![4]

The article established Adelman as a true pioneer in both choice of subject and method of analysis. Still, a tenure-track appointment eluded her and her frustration increased. She enjoyed working with colleagues at first-rate institutions, but continued to experience discrimination against women seeking full-time permanent appointments. Everyone recognized that her work was outstanding, but no tenure-track position was offered. Later, she wrote of the experience: 'The quantity and quality of my publication would have been sufficient to earn me a solid promotion to tenure in any first rate institution, had I been male. . . . The hardest thing during this period was to keep from getting bitter'.[5]

Her first book, *Theories of Economic Growth and Development*, also had a somewhat unique origin. It was written to be published as part of an undergraduate text on economic development, but the publisher rejected it as being at a more advanced level than the rest of the book. Not knowing exactly what to do with the material, she submitted it as a separate work to Stanford University Press. She noted later with some amusement that she had been told by her Marxist colleague Paul Baran that 'It's all very simple, Irma', and that she should 'let the market decide' on its merits.[6] The book, which was published by Stanford University Press, and received favourable reviews, highlighted one of her lifetime research interests. She wrote subsequently:

> This book . . . set the stage for one of my consistent lines of research; how the economic growth of nations is affected by and, in turn, affects economic and political institutions and sociocultural structures and values; and how institutions and economic structures and choices affect the diffusion of benefits from economic and institutional change. I felt the need to understand these processes better and to base my understanding on empirically generated hypotheses and stylized facts.[7]

On another occasion Adelman explained why institutional arrangements and the potential for economic growth were related. In response to the question, 'Why are some countries wealthy and others poor?' she answered:

> Historically, what mattered was whether a country had sufficient institutional development to benefit from the Industrial Revolution. Those countries that did not have the institutional conditions – either because of colonialism (e.g. India) or because of backwardness (e.g. Russia) – were unable to benefit from the revolution in technology. It was not a question of natural resources; in fact, most developing countries are, on the average, resource-rich rather than resource-poor. Even now, differences in economic developing countries are much more a matter of institutional development policy choices. . . .[8]

To the question of what institutions these might be, she responded, 'Institutions that allow for factor mobility and political institutions that allow for a choice of policies that would be beneficial to the development of a modern industrial base'.[9]

As circumstances in her career changed, so did Adelman's opinion of the traditional view. Adelman and her husband moved to Washington, DC, in 1962 and there she met her lifetime collaborator, Cynthia Taft Morris. Both were research associates at the Brookings Institutions. Of Morris, Adelman wrote later, 'we both had just moved to Washington, following, like the Biblical Ruth, our husbands' careers, and were both a little disoriented by the need to build new professional bases for ourselves'.[10] Both Morris and Adelman worked part-time in the summer of 1962 at the Agency for International Development (AID) in the research division headed by Hollis Chenery.

What they found at AID was a data source previously unutilized for development studies; these were the AID country reports – monographs generated by AID offices in the field and sent to Washington as annual reports on their respective countries. She and Morris were the first economists to use these as a basis for research. Adelman wrote, 'They were treasure-troves of up to date information on industry, agriculture, investment and international trade . . . an invaluable starting point'.[11]

Here was the raw material Adelman wanted to find on interactions of the economic, social and political aspects of economic development. This fount of information was to be married to a statistical technique she discovered in the psychological literature – factor analysis. She became very excited about the possibility of combining the two in exploratory research on interactions about which there were no validated theories. This was a major change in methodology in the field of economic development. Instead of constructing hypotheses deductively and then searching for confirming data, she proposed to let available data suggest appropriate theories and hypotheses. These in turn could be tested and refined. Her particular use of this 'continual feed' technique, together with the factor analysis, can be likened to a 'thunder-clap' in the profession when it later became known. The results of the new data and statistical techniques were published as *Society, Politics, and Economic Development – A Quantitative Approach*.[12]

At this time, Adelman and most of the economics profession believed that economic growth was beneficial to all. This was the 'received doctrine' or collective wisdom, consistent with the adage 'a rising tide lifts all boats'. In Washington, Adelman and Morris had come to question the 'trickle-down' theory – the idea that, when all is said and done, improvements in well-being due to development will accrue to all citizens, even those at lower income levels. She wrote:

> I believed with the mainstream in the trickle down [theory]. I thought that there might be some time lags, but the time lags would be of an acceptable magnitude. Lo and behold we did that study and found that it wasn't so and this caused a great trauma for me. I had chosen economic development in order to help people and I wasn't helping the people I wanted to help.[13]

It's not that the subject of the functional distribution of income was a new topic. The long-term impact of economic growth on the distribution of income has been a concern of economists since the nineteenth century. The study of the functional distribution of income was investigated by both Ricardo and Marx. Ricardo's model predicted that workers' and capitalists' shares of the national product would fall as that of landlords rose. Marx predicted a polarization of society when workers and small capitalists were pushed toward subsistence wages while the largest capitalists had high profits and very large incomes. Hence Adelman and Morris' concern about income shares and distributive justice during the development process was not new; what was new was their approach to the subject. They proposed to develop their investigation by study of actual experience as shown in real world data.

Little previous theorizing had been done about the size distribution among individuals. Some conclusions about the effects of industrialization on income had been proposed, particularly emphasizing the effect of such variables as occupation, wealth and education. No major research on time series data over decades had ever appeared and comparisons between countries were few. One exception to this wholesale omission of income distribution effects was in the work of Simon Kuznets. Kuznets speculated that in the industrially advanced countries the distribution of income may have narrowed over the twentieth century. For underdeveloped nations the opposite might be true – income distribution may have widened as Gross Domestic Product rose.[14] Thus, Adelman and Morris's research question was very well defined: what effect did the process of economic growth have on the distribution of individual incomes, particularly on those near the bottom of the economic ladder?

The research on the distribution question led Adelman to a pair of extremely important journal articles in which she chided earlier development economists for not recognizing their errors. The first appeared in the *Journal of Development Economics* in 1974.[15] Boldly, she wrote, 'It has thus become clear that the economic development processes of the fifties and sixties have not led to the intended result – massive improvements in the welfare of the poor – but have, if anything, increased inequality'.[16] She asked further, 'How is it that processes that lead to the further immiseration of the poor could take place virtually unnoticed by the intellectual leaders of the mainstream of the field of economic development?'[17]

She blamed the failure of development economics on four deficiencies in the approach taken by the great majority of development economists:

1) the failure to take a sufficiently broad view of the development process,
2) the failure to monitor results adequately,
3) the pervasive search for panaceas and for simplicity and simple guidance rules,
4) Insufficient humility and insufficient professionalism in our approach to development.[18]

For a woman who had had difficulty even securing a permanent academic appointment, this was a powerful broadside at the professional dreadnoughts.

Adelman urged remediation through taking the following steps:

1) Return to the grand economics of Marx and Schumpeter, but use the empirical, analytical and mathematical techniques available today.
2) Put more effort into scientific measurement (not into data collection).
3) Immerse technically well-trained individuals in dynamically oriented case studies at the micro level.
4) Do not make a fetish of simplicity.
5) Try to keep an open and sensitive mind.
6) Finally, do your damndest and keep your fingers crossed.[19]

In the second piece, a path breaking article in the *American Economic Review*, Adelman again called into question the idea that some goals of development, such as greater equity, were positively correlated with economic growth.[20] She reviewed her previous findings based on data for 43 underdeveloped countries. This was a remarkably large sample, given the paucity of the data – surely it was a tribute to her determination to use real world statistics. Her study had traced the experience of the poorest 60 per cent of income receivers, compared with a measure of various aspects of a nation's economic, social and political performance. The conclusion was most significant:

> We found that for the longest part of the development process . . . the primary impact of economic development on income distribution is, on the average, to decrease both the absolute and the relative incomes of the poor. Not only is there no automatic trickle-down of the benefits of development; on the contrary, the development process leads typically to a trickle-up in favor of the middle class and the rich.[21]

In *Economic Growth and Social Equity in Developing Countries*, she and Morris wrote:

> We found that the share of income accruing to the poor first declines rapidly, then less rapidly, and then, depending on the policy choices made, either levels off (the reverse J) or starts increasing (the U). Politically, as the indigenous middle class and urbanization improve, the influence on policy of non-elite groups starts extending to the middle class and to workers in the modern sector. But we found that the greater political participation of these groups does not redound to the benefit of the poor.[22]

Adelman's results meant that at least for a substantial portion of the development process there was a trade-off between economic development and an increase in the economic well-being of the poor. The results proved that an increase in GDP did not guarantee there would be improvements in the position of those near the bottom of the income distribution. By the time this article appeared, Adelman had advanced on the university career ladder, but the peaks in the profession were still held by men with a more benign view of the development process. Cautiously, she wrote of the technique by which she and Morris reached their conclusions:

> Were it not for the function-free statistical technique we adopted for our study, and were it not for our inductive empirical approach, we would have adopted an *a priori* specification confirming the modernization-cum-trickle-down theories. We would then have ascribed the poor statistical fit to poor data and small sample size.[23]

Worried about the consequences of publishing their conclusions, Adelman and Morris delayed publication for two years because 'we feared that our findings would be used as an argument to curtail resources for foreign-assistance rather than direct resources to more poverty-oriented projects and programmes'.[24]

Eager to show how these results could be applied to the real world, Adelman participated in the construction of a sophisticated income distribution planning model. The model was designed to explore how certain economic instruments – taxes, transfers, factor prices – affected income distribution. It introduced a modified general equilibrium approach and to solve the model a tâtonnement (auction) occurred at each step. Thus, short-run income distribution was the result of production and consumption decisions in a price-flexible model.

The model Adelman constructed with Sherman Robinson was tested on South Korean data.[25] The result was remarkable. Adelman wrote, 'Some indication of the validity of the model may be inferred from the fact that the base period solution for the model reproduced the 1968 data within less than 1 per cent for every one of the approximately 2000 endogenous variables'.[26] Her suggested conclusion was that 'while one can make small gains in the welfare of the poor through large changes within the system, the goal of equity cannot be achieved without radical reform'.[27] Tinkering 'just won't achieve much improvement and further, policy instruments that are most effective in improving income distributions are different from those that are best for raising economic growth rates'.[28] Consequently, both timing and choice of goals were important in any successful development plan.

Adelman called her own proposal depauperization. Her recommendations were based on both economic and moral considerations, and she wrote:

> the proper long-term goal of national development policy must be successive relaxation of the systematic obstacles to the full realization of the human potential of its members. The goals of economic development are then twofold: to provide the material basis for achieving these objectives and to establish the economic conditions for relaxing other barriers to self-realization (access to education, work satisfaction, status, security, self-expression and power).[29]

She recognized that some temporary sacrifices in the national economic growth rate might have to be made to achieve greater equity and that all components of her overall objective might not be attained simultaneously. She explained, 'the ultimate realization of depauperization is likely to require appropriately phased sequences of economic strategies, each aimed at optimizing some subset of the total goal package'.[30] Here was an ambitious, radical and comprehensive proposal that the rest of the profession greeted with some scepticism.

To support her programme, Adelman cited the post-World War II experience of five non-Communist countries: Israel, Japan, South Korea, Singapore and Taiwan. She believed these countries had successfully combined the goals of accelerated growth and improvements in the income of the poor. She examined the timing of policy strategies. Two extreme strategies for depauperization were possible: grow now, redistribute and educate later; or, redistribute and educate now, grow later. She generalized her preference as follows:

> Stage I: Radical asset redistribution, focusing primarily on land
> Stage II: Massive accumulation of human capital, far in excess of current demand for skills.
> Stage III: Rapid, human-resource-intensive growth.[31]

To delay asset redistribution or to choose growth first would lead to unsuccessful results in terms of equity. Based on these findings, Adelman came to advocate development plans where redistribution and human capital accumulation were primary considerations.

As Adelman's work had proceeded, so had her career. Her first permanent appointment was at Johns Hopkins University, after which she moved to Northwestern University in Illinois. In 1972 she returned to Washington, the World Bank and the University of Maryland. In 1977 she accepted one of her most satisfying appointments, the Cleveringa chair at the University of Leyden in Holland. It was a rotating chair established by the Queen of the Netherlands to commemorate the resistance of Leyden University, led by Cleveringa, a law professor, to the Nazi order to fire all Jewish professors. In her inaugural address, 'Redistribution before growth – a strategy for developing countries', she reiterated the position she had taken in the *American Economic Review*. Afterward, she wrote:

> I advocated asset redistribution before, rather than after, improvements in the asset's productivity; land reforms before improvements in agricultural productivity and mass primary education before a major push on industrialization. Asset redistribution before improvements in productivity would enable growth promoting measures to go hand in hand with equity-improving measures, thereby greatly enhancing the potential for improving the lot of the poor through economic development.[32]

In 1979 Adelman received an offer from her alma mater, the University of California, Berkeley. The offer coincided with a change in her personal life and her divorce in 1980. She accepted the offer eagerly and looked forward to the study of the interaction between agricultural and industrial development. She now holds the Thomas Forsyth Hunt Chair in the Department of Agricultural and Resource Economics.

Adelman also returned to her work with Cynthia Taft Morris, begun in 1965 but published only in 1988. They prepared a historical study on the role that institutional and political forces had played in inducing the very diverse economic responses of individual countries to the early Industrial Revolution in Great Britain. Morris had gathered comparable information on 23 countries for the period 1850–1914. As an economic historian with an institutional interest, she was finally persuaded to put her name as first author. The book appeared as *Comparative Patterns of Economic Development, 1850–1914*.[33]

Adelman and Morris extended their research for the book into a remarkable journal article in *World Development*, entitled 'Nineteenth-century-development experience and lessons for today'.[34] In the article they reviewed the findings presented in the book and discussed their relevance for the twentieth century's developing countries. They designed a special components technique for the research, using 35 institutional and economic variables applied to 23 countries and three time periods, to answer the question, 'What lessons might our historical results have for today?'[35]

What they found were great complexity and diversity in the development process for countries at dissimilar levels of development and direction. Many factors determined a country's particular path of change, such as the size of the agricultural surplus, land tenure arrangements, export opportunities, technology and demographic conditions. Arching over all, however, was the effect of institutions: institutions were major determinants of both the pace and the structure of economic growth. While countries followed different patterns of change, they observed that sustained, widespread growth did not take place without favourable governmental and political policies. Further, a wide pattern of land holdings and favourable incentives to produce in both the agricultural and industrial sectors were required. Literacy, transportation and political participation also mattered, but institutions were most important. Adelman and Morris concluded that 'political institutions and land institutions matter most – political institutions because they determine policy and land institutions because they determine agriculture's multifaceted contributions to economic development'.[36] Hence, countries with widely held landholdings and relatively high literacy rates, such as Denmark and Switzerland, were likely to experience long-term economic development. Countries where large landholdings were held by non-tilling elites and peasants were poor and uneducated, such as Argentina, did not experience strong, widely diffused economic growth. Here was historical evidence that confirmed what Adelman and Morris had recommended for the twentieth century: redistribute and educate first and grow later. How immensely satisfied they must have been to see how these findings dovetailed with their earliest recommendations.

Adelman's work has continued to explore strategies for economic development and structural adjustment, emphasizing equity and institutional change. One such study concerned the response of Mexico to its debt crisis of the 1980s.[37] Mexico was a middle-income oil exporter and its response may illuminate the choices open to countries in similar circumstances. Adelman's study was performed to answer the question of whether the Mexican government, in response to its financial crisis, could have chosen workable policies that were more equitable in terms of workers and the poor. Mexico chose an austerity programme – of cutting wages and subsidies – to reduce its balance of payments deficit. Given that nationwide measures had to be taken, had the government chosen that combination of measures least burdensome to the poorest households?

Adelman and Taylor's study included four counterfactual policy experiments using policy alternatives. Because of the special modelling techniques she had developed, she was able to perform 'experiments', using various assumption combinations. She was able to trace what was likely to have happened in the economy in each of the scenarios. It was a very powerful and revealing methodology.

Central to the government's strategy had been a reliance on wage repression and subsidy reduction. Adelman studied the impact on income earners of all types, but she examined most closely the consequences for urban and rural workers and the poor. She found that there was a particularly heavy burden imposed on low income groups and that resulting poverty among households was 'staggering'.

Other features of the government's policy response to the financial crisis were also examined. Mexico could not afford to increase its balance of payments deficit due to its debtor status. Adelman found that the policy of wage repression led to only slightly better results from the government's point of view than could have been obtained without the policy. Another factor analysed was foreign leakage of income – the phenomenon of capital flight. The government had claimed that strong wage restraint was necessary to minimize capital export by both nationals and investors. Hence, Adelman performed her experiments both with and without capital flight. The results showed that the country did better, of course, when capital flight did not take place. Whether it would actually have been possible to prevent, or mostly prevent, capital flight from taking place without strong wage restraint remained open to speculation.

Adelman concluded that 'the main culprit in Mexico's disastrous economic performance of the 1980s has been the choice of wage-repression policies, as an international debt-repayment mechanism'.[38] Further, 'wage repression is clearly a drastic remedy for achieving a balance of trade surplus'.[39] Instead, she found agricultural development was the key to successful macroeconomic adjustment policies. The study results supported the case for 'agricultural development-led industrialization (ADLI)'.[40] The path actually chosen by the Mexican government 'may have exacerbated their economic crisis' and was unduly harsh.[41] Finally, she concluded that 'adjustment with a more human face is possible' and that a different mix of policies would have been less burdensome.[42]

Adelman and various collaborators have continued to advocate equity-oriented development strategies. They have analysed policy options for different time periods and various countries. Their evidence supports the original conclusion that, for equitable results to occur, redistribution and education must be emphasized first with growth coming later. Adelman believes that the rest of the economics profession now recognizes the need for education at an early stage in the development process, whether countries practise the principle or not. She believes also that her advocacy of widespread asset redistribution, particularly in land, has been rejected as 'too radical'. Of the acceptance of her ideas she has written:

> With my change of emphasis in development policy towards income distribution and poverty, I lost all popularity with planning agencies in developing countries themselves. For a while, I was popular with international agencies with a policy orientation: the ILO [International Labour Organization] and the World Bank, in particular. But as their interest shifted towards debt and trade problems, this policy involvement stopped as well. What policy influence I now have is indirect: through my academic research and policy writings.[43]

In retrospect, she is particularly proud of her advisory work to the government of South Korea during the 1964–1973 period. Here her ideas made a genuine difference to the economic policies chosen. Of the experience she wrote:

> the strategy of labor-intensive, export-led economic growth incorporated in Korea's Second Five Year Plan, the design of which I led, was not one that president Park initially wanted. He wanted the 'export-led' component but would have preferred capital-intensive basic industries to labor-intensive ones. I persuaded the deputy prime minister of the superiority of stressing labor-intensive industries (on comparative advantage and income distribution grounds) and he, in turn, persuaded the president citing large unemployment and student demonstrations.[44]

For her work she received a Presidential decoration and citation which reads:

> With deep interest in the wellbeing of the Korean people. Mrs Irma Adelman, the professor at Northwestern University, has devoted her efforts with superb competence to the economic development of the Republic of Korea and thereby greatly contributed towards attaining the goals of economic self-sufficiency pursued by the Government of the Republic of Korea. Her valuable donation and service has gained for her the appreciation and admiration of the Korean people.[45]

Her current professional interests include:

1) Income distribution and poverty in developing countries.
2) Economic development and institutional change.
3) Industrial and agricultural policy in developing countries.
4) Economic planning and operations research.
5) International trade and economic development.

Yet, her works include a much broader collection of topics. Her major articles have been published in two volumes, making it easier for readers to access and appreciate her work. She takes great satisfaction in supervising student research and in the work of her former students. Residing in a delightful home overlooking the San Francisco Bay area, she enjoys a rewarding personal and professional life. Lest it be thought that she has completed her work, she continues to look for answers and says, with zest, 'I live and breathe economics!'

Notes

1. Arnold, Roger A. (1992), 'Interview: Irma Adelman', *Economics*, 2nd edn, St Paul, Minnesota: West Publishing Co., pp. 809–10.
2. Adelman, Irma (1961), *Theories of Economic Growth and Development*, Stanford, California: Stanford University Press.
3. Adelman, Irma and Frank Adelman (1959), 'The dynamic properties of the Klein–Goldberger model', *Econometrica*, pp. 596–625.
4. Adelman, Irma (1989), 'Confessions of an incurable romantic', in J.A. Kregel (ed.), *Recollections of Eminent Economists*, vol. **2**, New York; New York University Press, p. 132.
5. Adelman (1989), p. 144.
6. Adelman (1989), p. 133.
7. Adelman (1989), p. 155.
8. Arnold (1992), pp. 809–10.
9. Arnold (1992), pp. 809–10.
10. Adelman (1989), p. 133.
11. Adelman (1989), p. 134.
12. Adelman, Irma and Cynthia Taft Morris, (1967), *Society, Politics, and Economic Development – A Quantitative Approach*, Baltimore: Johns Hopkins University Press.
13. Adelman, interview, 5 November, 1993.
14. Adelman, Irma and Cynthia Taft Morris (1973), *Economic Growth and Social Equity in Developing Countries*, Stanford, California: Stanford University Press, pp. 133–4.
15. Adelman, Irma (1974), 'On the state of development economics', *Journal of Development Economics*, 1: pp. 3–5.
16. Adelman (1974), p. 3.
17. Adelman (1974), p. 3.
18. Adelman (1974), p. 4.
19. Adelman (1974), pp. 4–5.
20. Adelman, Irma (1975), 'Development economics – a reassessment of goals', *American Economic Review*, (May), p. 302.
21. Adelman (1975), p. 302.
22. Adelman, Irma and Cynthia Taft Morris (1973), *Economic Growth and Social Equity in Developing Countries*, Stanford, California: Stanford University Press. Quoted

from J.A. Kriegel, (ed.) (1989), *Recollections of Eminent Economists*, Vol. 2, New York: New York University Press.

23. Adelman (1989), p. 136.
24. Adelman (1989), p. 136.
25. Adelman, Irma and Sherman Robinson (1978), *Income Distribution Policy in Developing Countries: The Case of Korea*, Stanford, California: Stanford University Press.
26. Adelman (1975), p. 305.
27. Adelman (1975), p. 305.
28. Adelman (1975), p. 303.
29. Adelman (1975), p. 306.
30. Adelman (1975), p. 306–7.
31. Adelman (1975), p. 308.
32. Adelman (1989), p. 140.
33. Morris, C.T. and Irma Adelman (1988), *Comparative Patterns of Economic Development*, Baltimore: Johns Hopkins University Press.
34. Morris, C.T. and Irma Adelman (1989) 'Nineteenth century development experience and lessons for today', *World Development* **17**(9), pp. 1417–32.
35. Morris and Adelman (1989), p. 1418.
36. Morris and Adelman (1989), p. 1429.
37. Adelman, Irma and J.E. Taylor (1990), 'Is structural adjustment with a human face possible? The case of Mexico', *Journal of Development Studies*, **26**(3), pp. 387–407.
38. Adelman and Taylor (1990), p. 406.
39. Adelman and Taylor (1990), p. 406.
40. Adelman and Taylor (1990), p. 406.
41. Adelman and Taylor (1990), p. 400.
42. Adelman and Taylor (1990), p. 406.
43. Adelman (1989), p. 257.
44. E-mail: Adelman to Polkinghorn, 12 March 1998.
45. Kriegel, J.A. (ed.) (1989), *Recollections of Eminent Economists*, Vol. 2, New York, New York University Press, pp. 142–3.

8 Barbara Bergmann (1927—)

Born in what she called the 'sour-cream soaked Bronx', Barbara Bergmann grew up in a community long known for its willingness to question the beliefs of others. It was a community where differences of opinion were voiced loudly and often; some in the economics profession believe that Bergmann has continued in that tradition throughout her career.

She was a scholarly child who was interested in mathematics. Subsequently she attended Cornell University, where she studied mathematics and then became interested in economics. She obtained her bachelor's degree in 1948 and then applied to Cornell and to Harvard for graduate school. Flying in the face of what some would call 'true' economics, she chose Harvard when Cornell had offered a full scholarship and Harvard had offered none. She felt her preparation inadequate in economics, so prior to her enrolment she went through Kenneth Boulding's undergraduate textbook 'with a fine tooth comb'.

There were two courses in economic theory at Harvard, one from Edward Chamberlin and one from Vassily Leontieff. Those students who were well prepared for graduate study spurned Chamberlin's course which covered Marshall's *Principles* and his own *Monopolistic Competition*. Bergmann, however, was quite impressed with this course, partially because some of it was new to her and also because Chamberlin considered subjects which could not be described well by the more formal theories. Later she took Leontieff's course and enjoyed it as well. She associated with students such as Dale Jorgenson and Richard Caves and Alice Rivlen. In choosing a dissertation topic, Bergmann confessed that 'she floundered'. She was somewhat mystified as to how to proceed because she wasn't entirely sure what economists 'did'. She had a few ideas, which she discussed with others, but was not encouraged. Later, she worked on the consumption portion of the New York Metropolitan Region Study, 1957–61, and part of this became her topic. It was not one that inspired her, but she finished relatively quickly. She developed a forecasting model and said that she wrote the rest of the framework for the dissertation 'in a cafe in about three nights'.[1]

She took a teaching position at Brandeis University, where she failed to get tenure, and associated herself with the Brookings Institution. It was her departure for Washington which occasioned her acquaintance with her future husband, Fred Bergmann. Before leaving for Washington, she encountered another economist at a party and discussed the fact that she was moving. The friend remembered that he had had a recent letter from a friend of his who mentioned that he hadn't found Washington very enjoyable because he had met few women. The economist wrote to his Washington friend, giving him the names of two women who were expecting to move to the city. Barbara's name was first, so Fred called her for a date. They were married in a relatively short time.

Meanwhile her career proceeded more smoothly. She had learned the lesson of how economists work, which had eluded her at Harvard. Her publications multiplied quickly, as she pursued her interest in applied economics. In her well known 1971 article in the *Journal of Political Economy*, she investigated the effects on white incomes of changes in the proportion of black–white employment in certain occupations. In the paper she examined the racial make-up of a number of occupational categories to determine whether black males were to be found in predictable numbers. In the nineteenth century, F.Y. Edgeworth had compared numbers of persons in particular occupations with their numbers in the general population to explain differences in wages. Bergmann's technique was more sophisticated. She asked whether blacks were to be found in an occupation based upon the number of them having the required educational credentials.

Using 1960 census data on employment of males by race, she separated the studied occupations into three categories: occupations where blacks were under-represented, equally represented or over-represented. She described the phenomenon of 'occupational crowding', a concept she was able to utilize extensively in her research. In the summary, she described the problem succinctly: 'Discrimination concentrates Negroes into certain occupations while virtually excluding them from others. In the occupations to which Negroes are relegated, marginal productivity may be lowered by the enforced abundance of supply'.[2]

In addition to establishing the fact of overcrowding in a limited number of occupations, Bergmann explored the economic consequences of discrimination and estimated the size of gains and losses that might occur in the future if integration of employment were to take place. Contrary to the sizable losses in white incomes and in the rate of economic growth predicted by opponents of change, Bergmann predicted that costs would be small. Only the whites with minimal education would be impacted; she projected they might experience a one-time loss as large as ten per cent. On all other whites and on national income, the effect was estimated to be trivial. Blacks would benefit by small gains. All in all, she found a lessening of discrimination would have a small positive monetary effect for blacks – not the chaotic and costly labour market adjustment feared by proponents of the status quo.

This paper inspired Bergmann and others to continue to study the subject. One of these studies concerned differences in occupational standing of black Americans relative to whites by industry and area.[3] The conclusion drawn was that differences in status were better predicted by differences in promoting non-discriminatory behaviour than by differences in education, transportation or other factors. The implication was that the federal government should make a larger effort to enforce existing laws against discrimination in employment.

With that foundation, Bergmann joined William Krause in preparing a model for further study of integration in employment.[4] It was a mathematical formulation of the dynamics of the integration process, intended to forecast the changes in the proportions of blacks and whites that would result if blacks were hired into vacancies achieved by normal labour turnover and growth. Once the model was developed it could be used to evaluate the efforts and successes of firms and industries in achieving integration. On the basis of the results obtained, two questions could be answered: 1) Will a continuation of current hiring practices result in a reasonable degree of integration in a specified period of time? and 2) If the answer to the first question is no, how do current practices have to be changed? Thus, a formulation was created to evaluate actual situations with those that could be generated theoretically. Thus, court-ordered compliance instructions could move beyond the qualitative 'more' to the quantitative 'how much' – a very important step. Bergmann and Krause concluded that the progress of integration in employment had been 'glacial' and that change was occurring at an excruciatingly slow pace. They estimated that the hiring of blacks might have to be increased by more than five times if targeted progress were to be achieved.

In a subsequent article, Bergmann wrote, 'There are two phenomena associated with employment discrimination against blacks: 1) blacks are distributed among occupations differently from whites, even after differences in education are accounted for; and 2) within occupations, whites earn more than blacks do. The same two phenomena are observed as between men and women'.[5] From this analysis of racial discrimination in job markets, it was a short step to an investigation of the effects of sexual discrimination in employment.

Many economists, including Bergmann, think the most significant change in our economy in the post-1945 period has been the increase in female participation rates in the paid labour force. Bergmann has called it 'the greatest revolution of our time'[6] and set out to analyse it as a market phenomenon. Her effort culminated in *The Economic Emergence of Women*, a path-breaking book which changed the way people thought about the world around them. It was the economic rationale to accompany the moral argument for the equality of women in the workplace.

Bergmann began by arguing that gender roles have changed drastically from those observed in the past: women no longer devote a lifetime to care of the home and family. Men no longer may be able to provide an uninterrupted stream of income sufficient to support their families. Bergmann wrote 'We are witnessing the break-up of the ancient system of sex roles under which men were assigned a monopoly of access to money making and mature women were restricted to the home'.[7] Further, she argued that these changes are not of recent origin and are not accidental but are instead the result of long-term changes in family roles for men and women. She then proceeded to examine the reasons for her conclusion and, later, the implications of those changes. Contrary to the commonly held belief in the universality of the middle class full-time homemaker, she wrote, 'the move of women into paid work started modestly more than a century ago, and its origins go back at least two centuries'.[8] After a convincing presentation of the data, she turned to the underlying cause – the rising cost of earnings sacrificed by staying home. Other enabling changes also occurred, primarily the fall in the birth rate. Hence, both a 'push' and a 'pull' were occurring. The push was the reduction of hours necessary to produce required household products and services; the pull was the wage available outside the home. Wages were rising due to the increased productivity of labour. At the same time, the security of marriage was declining due to increased desertion and formal divorce. Women were no longer certain of lifelong support for themselves and their children.

It is a tribute to Bergmann's versatility that she dealt with the same topic in a lighter vein in another presentation. In 'The Economic Risks of Being a Housewife'[9] she considered the occupation of housewife as compared to other occupations. The dictionary definition of an occupation is 'an activity that serves as one's regular source of livelihood', and that makes a housewife a member of the largest single occupation in the United States. Thus, Bergmann wrote that, 'it is certainly both legitimate and interesting to compare the advantages and disadvantages of the housewife's source of livelihood with those of other sources'.[10]

In the article, she says that the housewife's occupational duties are well known; it is also well known that her 'job' may end at any time, either at her own discretion or at that of her husband. The displaced homemaker may find that she is leaving a full-time position of low status and that her alternatives are limited. Her circumstances may be awkward because of the difficulty of moving from one housewife job to another; there may be a period of unemployment between 'situations'. The 'live-in' feature of the housewife's job means that another residence must be found for the former housewife and perhaps accompanying children. Considerable capital may be required both for the move and any investment the woman might make to improve her chances of finding further employment, either as a homemaker or in another occupation. If she wishes to leave the marriage but can't afford it, she may face physical abuse and more. Either a threat to leave by the husband or his actual departure increases fear of 'job termination' and lowers satisfaction with an 'intact' marriage. Bergmann writes, 'thus, the increasingly well known risk of a bad outcome has the effect of reducing the value of a "good" outcome'.[11] All in all, she concludes it is a risky business, and it is not surprising that currently married women might hedge their bets and seek paid work outside the home as insurance.

The second section of *The Economic Emergence of Women* dealt with women's experience in the labour market. Many employers were reluctant to hire women, thinking that jobs should be reserved for men 'as they had families to support'. In addition, employers and current male employees were hesitant about having women in their trades, perhaps because of the idea that the presence of women employees could disrupt the production process and ultimately reduce profits. The result was that women workers faced a great deal of discrimination in seeking employment. Most simply entered occupations that were already open to women. These occupations tended to offer lower wages and fewer benefits.

Occupational crowding resulted in a large wage gap between men's and women's earnings. There was an excess supply of workers to women's jobs. Bergmann wrote, 'Women's exclusion from some jobs pushes them into a labour market separate from men, a fenced-off market in which supply and demand decree low rates of pay'.[12] The wage gap between men and women persisted over many decades and through many changes in economic conditions.

Bergmann proposed that discrimination in the workplace and the pay gap be reduced by vigorous enforcement of equal opportunity laws and regulations. She also advocated a movement toward pay equity by the use of comparable worth policies. Minimum wage 'guidelines' in female occupations might also be set that would reflect human capital differences in such aspects as skill, effort and responsibility between 'women's jobs' and those traditionally held by men. She predicted that such guidelines might eventually result in the wage patterns found in a non-discriminatory market in the long run. She argued that changes would be feasible and not particularly costly; the benefits would outweigh the costs.

Having analysed the problems faced by women in the labour market, Bergmann discussed the consequences for the families of those who had joined the labour force. The problem faced by women was the loss of almost all leisure time; they faced the 'doubleday' of both home and work. Surveys showed that other family members were reluctant to undertake household duties. The problem was intensified for female single parents, and Bergmann devoted an entire chapter to detailing their situation. Here she argued that society has such a strong interest in what happens to the children of these families that collective action should be taken to ensure their welfare. Citing the low rate of compliance with child support orders, she advocated a thorough-going reform of the child support system. The new system would include automatic payroll deductions and a minimum benefit for every child. All children would be eligible for some healthcare benefits and there would be special provisions for handicapped children. Subsidized day care for single parents who were employed or seeking work would be guaranteed.

From these proposals, Bergmann went on to investigate what a different, industrialized system of housework and childcare would be like. She cited examples in Sweden and Israel and let her imagination run. Bergmann wrote, 'The industrialization of child care and food services, and perhaps housecleaning services as well can be thought of as the ultimate episode – and the logical conclusion – of the process that began millennium ago'.[13] Recent evidence supports Bergmann's conclusion; for example, change in this direction can be seen in the near revolution in our dining habits over the last 25 years. Competing with home cooked meals are sellers of prepared food. McDonalds and 'The Colonel' are never more than a few blocks away. Americans have been free to buy or not to buy from commercial sellers, and there is ample evidence that 'Ronald McDonald' has won. Sales of food purveyors of all kinds have seen their sales double and triple; it is said that, on the average each American eats at McDonalds once a week and at another fast food restaurant one more time. Office workers bring fewer lunches from home and send 'faxes' to nearby food sellers at noontime.

The industrialization of other home production will surely continue into the future with more commercial childcare and enlargement of the 'infant industries' of commercial home cleaners and shoppers. Centralization of such services may result in more efficiency since not every home would require its own stock of equipment and there is every reason to believe that there are economies of scale in production of these services. If this description sounds familiar, it is because one group of the population has already tried similar schemes – the affluent elderly. Some retirement complexes provide all of these services and more. What is chosen by the elderly may indeed become the way of life for the rest of us as well.

Bergmann concluded the book with a twelve-point policy agenda to promote justice in the workplace, justice for single parents, and fairness in family life. These proposals, she believed, deserve our thought. The first five were targeted toward behaviour in the workplace and constituted a plea for fairness that all workers ought to be able to support:

1) Improve enforcement of fairness in placement and promotion
2) Realign wage rates based on comparable duties
3) End sex segregation in vocational and engineering education
4) End discrimination against part-time workers
5) Campaign against sexual harassment.

Three special measures were put forth to aid the growing numbers of single-parent families:

6) National adoption of a deduction based, uniform child support plan
7) Set up special unemployment insurance for single parents
8) Establish a publicly funded, high quality child care system.

The last four proposals concerned family life:

9) Lower standard hours of daily work
10) Establish subsidies for apartment complexes with resident child-care facilities
11) Establish a new ethic of sharing family-care work between men and women
12) Help families with an impaired child by an insurance fund.[14]

Bergmann did not imagine that every reader would agree with these proposals. What she hoped was that readers would consider these suggestions carefully, debate them, and support those to which they attached high priority.

The Economic Emergence of Women was Bergmann's magnum opus. She placed it at the top of her best work.[15] The book was a great success when it appeared and it continues to be read today. It is less radical than it was in 1986, but no less relevant.

Her second major contribution to be considered here was on a very different topic: the focus and methodology of economics. Like Irma Adelman, Bergmann criticized the techniques, reasoning and inference of neoclassical economists. She took issue with those who believed that 'Thinking like an economist involves *using chains of deductive reasoning* in conjunction with *simplified models* to illustrate economic phenomena'.[16] This is the method of elegant abstraction, and Bergmann believed it was the wrong approach to finding things out in economic science. An example may clarify the difference between this neoclassical position and Bergmann's own. Suppose that we wish to determine how producers set output levels in a very competitive market. The neoclassical economist would construct a model by deduction and then infer from the model how producers must act, given the initial assumptions. Bergmann thought the approach should be direct: economists should just go out and ask business people how they determine output. While the difference appears small in this simplified example, it is much more substantial in real world situations.

In Bergman's eyes a typical professor remained at his desk, sequestered from the business community, musing on how he thought people might behave. He projected his singular theories and simplified them down to his own abilities, making certain that the variables included were defined in such a way that they could be found to be statistically significant. If his mathematical machinations failed to generate the desired results, he tossed them out and substituted other variables that came closer to what he has previously decided must be correct. Cloistered from the world outside, he was free to propose hypotheses that a rational person would reject at first hearing.

In an interview, Bergmann related the following example of how this methodology led to wrong conclusions:

> For years and years credit cards had 18 ½% interest rates [that] never varied, although the bank rate is one of the most volatile in the economy. There are few prices that are that volatile in terms of percentage. Yet here was this high interest rate that never varied. There was an article written by a professor at Northwestern who evolved a theory about it. It was the usual way that economists evolve theories, which is to sit in their offices and think about the phenomenon. His theory was that there was no competition in terms of interest rates ... because consumers were not interested in interest rates. When you take out a credit card – according to him – you never think you are going to put any credit on it. You think you are going to pay it off right away.
>
> Well, when I read that article I thought it was a bunch of s—t, that can't be right. About a year after I read that article, there was a change and some of the companies did start competing on the basis of rate. And it turned out

> that consumers were very interested. What happened was that some of the companies allowed people to transfer their [existing] balances. So I've got $10,000 on it on which I am paying 18 ½% and maybe I can transfer it and pay 12%, which is a huge saving. His theory was totally wrong. The typical economist's way of thinking about it [economics] or methods of finding out about it are totally inadequate. In my view you would have to go around and try to get people's comments and then you wouldn't make such a big mistake as saying people didn't care how high interest rates were.[17]

What does Bergmann think we ought to be doing? Her suggestions were very direct:

> If we are to build an economic science, we need first of all to gather knowledge about actual decision making. Second, we need to gather information about the conventions that are observed when the economic agents interact. Third, we need a rigorous way of computing the progression from micro decision systems to micro interactions, and then from the interactions to the macro results.[18]

Bergmann also explored the question of why economists continue to use models that do not add to our knowledge of the economy. She wrote, 'a . . . reason economists do not make personal and direct observations is that we have never done so, do not have a tradition of doing so; and do not know how to do so'.[19]

Since some economists have called for a change in methodology for many years, why is it that so little progress has been made? Bergmann suggested some reasons:

> It is unlikely that large numbers of economists will change their habits soon. Older economists are proud of the intellectual rigor of traditional economics, and have chosen the field because its deductive methodology is congenial to them. Many will be unwilling to consider seriously unfamiliar modes of research for which they have no training. For young economists, with careers to establish and older professors to impress, new methods look risky and time consuming. In order for a reform of economists' research methodology to gather steam, at least two or three of the leading academic departments must become centers of new forms of economic research on business behavior.[20]

She believed that we need to put aside this 'musing/regression' methodology and walk out of our offices to observe the world of economic reality. Instead of assuming away difficulties, we should utilize the new communication technologies to observe regularities of behaviour that actually occur, so that policy prescriptions are grounded in models incorporating the 'complexity of economic reality'.[21] Should any reader fail to understand, she added, 'We will never kill the silliness and confusion and fruitless controversy that the musing/regression methodology breeds unless something better is substituted'.[22] She continued, 'A turn is in order to methods which are less intellectually flashy, which are easier, more tractable and more productive'.[23]

Bergmann followed her own advice to communicate with business people in the real world. She wrote more than 15 columns in the early 1980s for the Sunday business section of the *New York Times*. The columns were written in a popular and accessible style and on topics in which the intelligent reader would be interested. The subjects addressed were as diverse as interest rates, deregulation, social security and professional sports unions. Two topics, covered briefly in these short articles, were developed into full-length books in the nineties. These were *In Defense of Affirmative Action* and *Saving Our Children From Poverty: What the United States Can Learn From France.*

In Defense of Affirmative Action was a most appropriate title for Bergmann's 1996 book.[24] She recognized that there was much opposition and reduced support in the country for such policies. Opponents of affirmative action claimed that these programmes based hiring on group rights rather than on individual qualifications. Bergmann, however, believed that affirmative action promoted justice in the workplace by encouraging consideration of entry-level applicants by merit and not by implicit racist or sexist policies. She also believed that if affirmative action policies were not retained, little progress could be made toward equal opportunity and fairness in the workplace. Lucrative careers would remain closed by discrimination; indeed, the situation in the workplace could worsen.

Whether fairness in hiring occurred depended upon the answer to the question, how do employers choose new employees? Do they consider hiring people of both sexes and all races? Or do they limit consideration to those possible applicants who mirror the past hires and current employees? Do they assume automatically that current employees would prefer not to work with people of a different race or sex? Have they asked themselves whether categories of potential employees who were previously excluded might have qualifications that might open new markets, provide new services or otherwise increase profits? If the answer to these questions is no, then it can be concluded that discrimination in the workplace will not be lessened by normal turnover of employees.

If a past discrimination pattern was not eroded over time, Bergmann believed that affirmative action policies had to be retained. To her, that meant that employers must be required to consider a variety of potential employees by goals or quotas in hiring. Only groups where there had been large-scale discrimination in the past would need to benefit from the protection. To act otherwise would – as Bergmann recognized – make the labour market 'a balkanized nightmare'.[25] She did not address the question of compliance. Still, she was convinced that if we are to move to a society where every individual can try to 'be all that he/she can be', affirmative action or a similar policy would be needed.

At the same time she was writing the book on affirmative action, she was preparing a second book, *Saving Our Children From Poverty: What the United States Can Learn From France.*[26] The subject of parent/child poverty was one she had studied for many years. Bergmann had written elsewhere that single parent families in our society were the group most vulnerable to poverty. Most of these single parent families were headed by women – divorced, never-married, separated or widowed.

Many people would agree that growing up in a poor environment can disadvantage a child seriously. Such an upbringing is widely cited as leading to violence, crime, child abuse or further poverty. It has been government policy since the 1930s to raise living standards for poor families by transfer payments such as AFDC (Aid to Families with Dependent Children), Social Security and so forth. A considerable number of people have come to the opinion that parents in such families should seek employment outside the home, both to lessen the need for public support and to set an example for their children. For that to be possible, however, most families will need out-of-home child care. While such care may be costly, it may also provide more than custodial benefits for affected children, just as has occurred in the 'Headstart' programme.[27] Provision of private child care in licensed centres could also be increased; in the last three decades it has quadrupled and further expansion of the industry is certainly possible. This privately provided child care will be relatively expensive and some of the poor parents will require government help to pay for it. The questions of 1) how is the needed child care to be provided? and 2) who is to pay for it? are part of the much larger subject of family policy in America.

Bergmann was part of a research team under the auspices of the Child Care Action Campaign that investigated the French government's child protection programme. France has a relative income distribution similar to the United States and it has groups within the population that suffer marginalization due to ethnicity and national origin and who are prone to poverty and isolation. To minimize intergenerational poverty, the government adopted a comprehensive family protection programme that included free, high quality preschool child care for all children who were toilet trained. Some subsidization of private child care for infants was also made available. This was the equivalent of extending the rationale for public education to preschoolers. The government recognized that the benefits went far beyond simple education. They professed to believe that French culture and tradition were transmitted at an earlier age than before and 'that both the children and the nation of which the children are future citizens, benefits'.[28]

Bergmann asked: Could the French really afford this large-scale programme? Statistics indicated that they could, even though French per-capita income is about 80 per cent of that of the United States. Child-oriented programmes in France, which include income support, medical assistance, and housing benefits in addition to child care, make up only about ten per cent of all government spending. Less than five per cent of annual Gross Domestic Product is devoted to child-oriented programmes. It seemed that such a level of support was clearly within their means. The result has been that child poverty fell in France to approximately six per cent, less than one-third of the 21 per cent found in the United States. French children appear to enjoy a better standard of living and a better set of opportunities for their futures. In comparison, American programmes are most niggardly. Bergmann advocates programmes that are less timid and modest than the United States has adopted up to now. For her, an acceptable programme would allow families to 'live decently, through programs that encourage and enable work, and that help keep families together'.[29]

It would have been difficult to have covered all of Bergmann's publications here, but the extent of her range is clear. Throughout her career she maintained six commitments in her work. These were summarized recently in a session at the meetings of the Allied Social Science Associations dedicated to her accomplishments. The paper was presented by her friend and associate, Heidi Hartmann, who wrote:

> Barbara Bergmann's approach to economics, and to feminist economics, is characterized by several striking dimensions that differentiate her approach from that of most other economists.[30] [She has]:
>
> 1) A willingness to incorporate values into her analysis openly
> 2) A commitment to applied economics – economic analysis that supports policy change that will improve women's and children's lives
> 3) A commitment to empirical economics – to data collection and data analysis
> 4) A commitment to communication with the public
> 5) A commitment to the truth even if it challenges popular myths
> 6) A commitment to focus on how change can occur – to be positive, not defeatist.

The English author John Ruskin wrote, 'the first duty of a state is to see that every child born therein shall be housed, clothed, fed and educated, till it attains years of discretion'.[31] This is a statement with which Bergmann would find much agreement. Indeed, Bergmann has spent a career documenting injustices in the home, in labour markets, in the workplace and in our care of children. Not everyone wanted to hear these things; sometimes it seemed easier to do things as they had always been done. Other writers with different views made them known and criticized her positions as too radical or unrealistic. Bergmann does not suffer fools lightly and was not slow to defend herself, sometimes generating a new round of argument. It was said in the last century that a woman's first line of defence in case of attack was her hat pin. Had Bergmann lived in the high days of hat pins, she would have been an expert in their use. Her advocacy and defence of the less privileged and vulnerable in our society has been pointed, persistent and effective.

Notes

1. Bergmann, Barbara R. (1994a), interview, September 6, 1994.
2. Bergmann, Barbara R. (1971), 'The effect on white incomes of discrimination in employment', *Journal of Political Economy*, **79**(2), pp. 294–313. Quotation p. 294.
3. Bergmann, Barbara R. and Jerolyn Lyle (1971), 'The occupational standing of negroes by areas and industries,' *The Journal of Human Resources* **6**(4), pp. 411–33.
4. Bergmann, Barbara R. and William Krause (1972), 'Evaluating and forecasting progress in the racial integration of employment', *Industrial and Labor Relations Review*, pp. 399–409.
5. Bergmann, Barbara R. (1974), 'Occupational segregation, wages and profits when employers discriminate by race and sex', *Eastern Economic Journal*, **1**(2) and (3), pp. 103–10. Quotation p. 103.
6. Bergmann, Barbara R. (1986), *The Economic Emergence of Women*, New York: Basic Books. Quotation from jacket.
7. Bergmann (1986), p. 3.
8. Bergmann (1986), p. 3.
9. Bergmann, Barbara R. (1981), 'The economic risks of being a housewife', *American Economic Review*, **71**(2), pp. 81–6.
10. Bergmann (1981), p. 81.
11. Bergmann (1981), p. 84.
12. Bergmann (1986), p. 146.
13. Bergmann (1986), p. 275.
14. Bergmann (1986), p. 302–13.
15. Bergmann (1994a), interview, September 6, 1994.
16. McEachem, William A. (ed.,) (1994), *The Teaching Economist*, Issue 8, p. 1.
17. Bergmann, interview, September 6, 1994.
18. Bergmann, Barbara R. (1987), ' "Measurement" or finding things out in economics', *Journal of Economic Education*, pp. 193–4.
19. Bergmann, Barbara R. (1994b), 'Have economists failed?', *Proceedings of the Inaugural Convention of the Eastern Economic Association*, Albany, New York, October 27, p. 20.
20. Bergmann, Barbara R. (1982), 'The failures of a chair-bound science', *The New York Times*, December 12.
21. Bergmann (1987), p. 200.
22. Bergmann (1987), p. 198.
23. Bergmann, (1994b), p. 24.

24. Bergmann, Barbara R. (1996a), *In Defense of Affirmative Action*, New York: Harper Collins, Basic Books.
25. Bergmann, (1996a), p. 94.
26. Bergmann, Barbara R. (1996b), *Saving Our Children From Poverty: What the United States Can Learn From France*, New York: Russell Sage Foundation.
27. 'Headstart' is a current early childhood programme for children from poor families.
28. Quoted from Bergmann, Barbara R. 'Child care: The key to ending child poverty', a Princeton Conference Paper on Social Policies for Children, May 25–27, 1994, p. 20.
29. Bergmann (1996b), p. 11.
30. Hartmann, Heidi (1997) 'The economic emergence of women: Bergmann's six commitments', Meetings of the Allied Social Sciences Association, New Orleans, January 5, p. 1.
31. Ruskin, John (1891), 'Time and tide', *The Complete Works of John Ruskin*, vol. 14, Letter XIII, Philadelphia: Reuwee, Wattley & Walsh.

Bibliography

Chapter 1: Jane Marcet

American Monthly Magazine (1833), vol. 1.

Colvin, Christina (ed.) (1971), *Maria Edgeworth: Letters from England 1813–1844*, Oxford: Clarendon Press.

Hutchison, T.W. (1978), *On Revolutions and Progress in Economic Knowledge*, Cambridge: Cambridge University Press.

La Rive, August de (1859), 'Madame Marcet', *Bibliothèque Universelle de Genève*, (March).

Lee, Sidney, (ed.) (1899), *Dictionary of National Biography*, London: Smith, Elder & Co.

Macaulay, Thomas B. (1851), *Critical and Historical Essays*, London: Longman, Brown, Green and Longman.

Malthus, T.R. (1816), Letter to Jane Marcet, Marcet Collection, Archive Guy de Pourtalès, Etoy, Switzerland (August).

Malthus, T.R. (1833), Letter to Jane Marcet. Reprinted in Bette Polkinghorn (September 1986), 'An Unpublished Letter from Malthus to Jane Marcet', *American Economic Review*, **76**: 845–7.

Marcet, Jane [published anonymously] (1806), *Conversations on Chemistry*, 1st American edition, Philadelphia: James Humphreys.

Marcet, Jane (21 September 1816), Letter to Pierre Prevost, Archive of the Fondation Augustin de Candolle, Geneva, Switzerland.

Marcet, Jane [published anonymously] [1828], *Conversations on Political Economy; in which the Elements of that Science are Familiarly Explained*, 3rd edition, first published 1817, Boston: Bowles and Dearborn.

Marcet, Jane [published anonymously] (1826), *Conversations on Evidences of Christianity*, London: Longman, Rees, Orme, Brown, Green & Longman.

Marcet, Jane [published anonymously] (1833), *John Hopkins's Notions on Political Economy*, London: Longman, Rees, Orme, Brown, Green & Longman.

Marcet, Mrs, (1851), *Rich and Poor*, London: Longman, Brown, Green & Longman.

Thompson, E.P. (1964), *The Making of the English Working Class*, London: Victor Gollancz.

Chapter 2: Harriet Martineau

Blaug, Mark (1958), *Ricardian Economics: A Historical Study*, New Haven: Yale University Press.

Fletcher, Max, (1974), 'Harriet Martineau and Ayn Rand: Economics in the Guise of Fiction', *American Journal of Economics and Sociology*, **33**(4) (October).

Lee, Sidney (ed.) (1893), *Dictionary of National Biography*, London: Smith, Elder & Co.

Martineau, Harriet (1827), *The Rioters; or, a Tale of Bad Times*, Wellington, Shropshire: Houlston.

Martineau, Harriet (1827), *The Turn Out; or Patience the Best Policy*, Wellington, Shropshire: Houlston.

Martineau, Harriet, (1832), Letter to Jane Marcet (11 October), Marcet Collection, Archive Guy de Pourtales, Etoy, Switzerland.

Martineau, Harriet (1834), *Illustrations of Political Economy*, 9 vols, London: Charles Fox.

Martineau, Harriet (1877), *Autobiography, with Memorials by Maria Weston Chapman*, 3 vols, reprinted in Gaby Weiner (ed.) (1983), *Harriet Martineau's Autobiography*, 2 vols, London: Virago.

O'Donnele, M., (n.d.), 'On Female Education: An Example of Early Economic Thinking of Harriet Martineau', Lafayette, LA: (unpublished).

Pichanick, Valerie (1980), *Harriet Martineau: The Woman and Her Work, 1802–1876*, Ann Arbor: The University of Michigan Press.

Polkinghorn, Bette (1995), 'Jane Marcet and Harriet Martineau: Motive, market experience and reception of their works popularizing classical political economy' in Dimand, Dimand and Forget, (eds), *Women of Value*, Aldershot, UK: Edward Elgar.

Quarterly Review, (April–July 1833), vol. XLIX, p. 151.

Webb, R.K. (1960), *Harriet Martineau: A Radical Victorian*, New York: Columbia University Press.

Chapter 3: Millicent Fawcett

Caine, Barbara (1992), *Victorian Feminists*, Oxford: Oxford University Press.

Fawcett, Millicent Garrett (1870), *Political Economy for Beginners*, London: Macmillan & Co.

Fawcett, Millicent Garrett (1874), *Tales in Political Economy*, London: Macmillan & Co.

Fawcett, Millicent Garrett (1924), *What I Remember*, London: T. Fisher Unwin, Ltd.

Fawcett, Henry and Millicent Garrett Fawcett (1872), *Essays and Lectures on Social and Political Subjects*, London: Macmillan & Co.

Goldman, Lawrence (1989), *The Blind Victorian: Henry Fawcett and British Liberalism*, Cambridge: Cambridge University Press.

Levine, Phillippa (1990), *Feminist Lives in Victorian England*, Oxford: Basil Blackwell, Ltd.

Polkinghorn, Bette (1982), 'Political economy disguised as fanciful fables', *Eastern Economic Journal*, (April) **VIII** (2).

Polkinghorn, Bette (1993), 'Millicent Fawcett's contribution to economic education: political economy for beginners', (June) unpublished.

Rubinstein, David (1986), *Before the Suffragettes: Women's Emancipation in the 1890's*, Brighton, England: The Harvester Press, Ltd.

Chapter 4: Rosa Luxemburg

Cliff, Tony (1959), 'Rosa Luxemburg', *International Socialism*, nos (2) and (3).

Dunayevskaya, Roya (1982), *Rosa Luxemburg, Women's Liberation and Marx's Philosophy of Revolution*, New Jersey: Humanities Press.

Egger, Daniel (1987), Movie Review of 'Rosa Luxemburg: A Life' by Elizabieta Ettinger and Margarethe von Trotta, *The Nation*, (25 April), **244**, (4), p. 546.

Frolich, Paul (1972), *Rosa Luxemburg: Her Life and Work*, 1st English translation 1940, New York and London: Monthly Review Press.

Howard, Dick (ed.) (1971), *Selected Political Writings of Rosa Luxemburg*, New York: Monthly Review Press.

Luxemburg, Rosa (1951), *The Accumulation of Capital*, 2nd edition, first published 1913, London: Routledge and Kegan Paul, Introduction by Joan Robinson.

Nettl, J.P. (1966), *Rosa Luxemburg*, London: Oxford University Press, 2 vols.

Waters, Mary-Alice, (ed), (1970), *Rosa Luxemburg Speaks*, New York: Pathfinder Press.

Chapter 5: Beatrice Webb

Mackenzie, Norman (ed.) (1978), *The Letters of Sidney and Beatrice Webb*, 3 vols. Cambridge: Cambridge University Press.

Radice, Lisanne (1984), *Beatrice and Sidney Webb: Fabian Socialists*, New York: St Martin's Press.

Seymour-Jones, Carole (1992), *Beatrice Webb: A Life*, Chicago: Ivan R. Dee.

Thomson, Dorothy L. (1973), *Adam Smith's Daughters*, New York: Exposition Press.

Webb, Beatrice (1887), 'A Lady's View of the Unemployed . . .', *Pall Mall Gazette* (18 February).

Webb, Beatrice (October 1887), 'The Dock Life of East London', *Nineteenth Century*, vol. **XXIII**, pp. 483–99.

Webb, Beatrice (1891), *The Cooperative Movement in Great Britain*, 2nd edn (1899), London: Swan Sonnenschein.

Webb, Sidney and Beatrice Webb (1894), *The History of Trade Unionism*, revised edn (1920), London: Longmans, Green & Co.

Webb, Sidney and Beatrice Webb (1913), *Industrial Democracy*, Printed by the authors for the Trade Unionists of the United Kingdom.

Webb, Beatrice (1926), *My Apprenticeship*, London: Longmans, Green & Co.

Webb, Beatrice (1948), *Our Partnership*, Barbara Drake and Margaret Cole (eds), New York and London: Longmans, Green & Co.

Webb, Beatrice (1952), *Diaries, 1912–1924*, Margaret Cole (ed.), London and New York: Longmans, Green & Co.

Webb, Beatrice (1982), *The Diary of Beatrice Webb*, Norman and Jeanne Mackenzie, (eds), vol. **1**: 1873–1892, Cambridge, Mass: The Belknap Press.

Chapter 6: Joan Robinson

Chamberlin, Edward H (1933), *The Theory of Monopolistic Competition*, Cambridge, Mass.: Harvard University Press.

Hagen, E.E. (1968), *The Economics of Development*, Homewood, Illinois: Richard D. Irwin, Inc.

Keynes, J.M. (1930), *A Treatise on Money*, 2 vols, London: Macmillan & Co.

Keynes, J.M. (1936), *The General Theory of Employment, Interest and Money*, London: Macmillan & Co.

Robinson, Joan (1969), *The Economics of Imperfect Competition*, 2nd edition, first published 1933, London: Macmillan & Co.

Robinson, Joan (1953), *Essays in the Theory of Employment*, 2nd edition, first published 1937, Oxford: Basil Blackwell.

Robinson, Joan (1964), *An Essay on Marxian Economics*, 2nd edition, first published 1942, Oxford: Basil Blackwell.

Robinson, Joan (1965), *The Accumulation of Capital*, 2nd edition, first published 1951, London: Macmillan & Co.

Robinson, Joan and Dorothea Morison (1966), 'Beauty and the beast', in *Collected Economic Papers*, vol **1**, Oxford: Basil Blackwell, pp. 225–33.

Robinson, Joan (1961), *Exercises in Economic Analysis*, London: Macmillan & Co.

Robinson, Joan (1964), *Economic Philosophy*, first published 1962, Garden City, New York: Doubleday & Co.

Robinson, Joan (1963), *Essays in the Theory of Economic Growth*, 2nd edition, first published 1962, London: Macmillan & Co.

Robinson, Joan (1962), 'Marxism: religion and science', *Monthly Review* (December).

Robinson, Joan (1967), *Economics: An Awkward Corner*, New York: Pantheon Books.

Robinson, Joan (1970), *Freedom and Necessity*, London: George Allen & Unwin.

Robinson, Joan (1971), *Economic Heresies, Some Old-Fashioned Questions in Economic Theory*, New York: Basic Books.

Robinson, Joan (1972), 'The second crisis of economic theory', *The American Economic Review*: Proceedings of the Eighty-fourth Annual Meeting of the American Economic Association, New Orleans, Louisiana, December 27–29, 1971, **LXII** (2) May pp. 1–10.

Sraffa, Piero (1965), 'Prelude to a critique of economic theory', Collected Economic Papers, vol. **3**, p. 7.

Turner, Marjorie (1989), *Joan Robinson and the Americans*, London: M.E. Sharp, Letter of Phyllis Maurice to Marjorie Turner, postmarked 14 January 1988.

Chapter 7: Irma Adelman

Adelman, Irma and Frank Adelman (1959), 'The dynamic properties of the Klein–Goldberger model', *Econometrica*, pp. 596–625.

Adelman, Irma (1961), *Theories of Economic Growth and Development*, Stanford, CA: Stanford University Press.

Adelman, Irma and Cynthia Taft Morris (1967), *Society, Politics, and Economic Development – A Quantitative Approach*, Baltimore: Johns Hopkins University Press.

Adelman, Irma and Cynthia Taft Morris (1973), *Economic Growth and Social Equity in Developing Countries*, Stanford, CA: Stanford University Press.

Adelman, Irma (1974), 'On the state of development economics', *Journal of Development Economics*, 1: pp. 3–5.

Adelman, Irma (1975), 'Development economics – a reassessment of goals', *American Economic Review*, (May), pp. 302–9.

Adelman, Irma, and Sherman Robinson (1978), *Income Distribution in Developing Countries; The Case of Korea*, Stanford, California: Stanford University Press.

Adelman, Irma (1989), 'Confessions of an incurable romantic', in J.A.

Kriegel (ed.), *Recollections of Eminent Economists*, vol **2**, New York: New York University Press.

Adelman, Irma and J.E. Taylor (1990), 'Is structural adjustment with a human face possible? The case of Mexico', *Journal of Development Studies*, **26** (3), pp. 387–407.

Adelman, Irma (5 November 1993) Interview at Berkeley, CA, USA.

Arnold, Roger A. (1992), 'Interview: Irma Adelman', *Economics*, 2nd edn., St Paul: Minnesota: West Publishing Co. pp. 809–10.

Morris, C.T. and Irma Adelman (1988), *Comparative Patterns of Economic Development*, Baltimore: Johns Hopkins University Press.

Morris, C.T. and Irma Adelman (1989), 'Nineteenth century development experience and lessons for today', *World Development*, **17**(9), pp. 1417–32.

Chapter 8: Barbara Bergmann

Bergmann, Barbara (1971), 'The effect on white incomes of discrimination in employment', *Journal of Political Economy*, **79**(2), pp. 294–313.

Bergmann, Barbara and Jerolyn Lyle (1971), 'The occupational standing of negroes by areas and industries', *The Journal of Human Resources*, **6**(4), pp. 411–33.

Bergmann, Barbara (1974a), 'Occupational segregration, wages and profits when employers discriminate by race and sex', *Eastern Economic Journal*, **1** (2) and (3), pp. 103–10.

Bergmann, Barbara (1974b), 'Have economists failed?', *Proceedings of the Inaugural Convention of the Eastern Economic Association*, Albany, New York, 27 October.

Bergmann, Barbara (1981), 'The economic risks of being a housewife', *American Economic Review*, **71**(2), pp. 81–6.

Bergmann, Barbara (1982), 'The failures of a chair-bound science', *The New York Times*, December 12.

Bergmann, Barbara (1986), *The Economic Emergence of Women*, New York: Basic Books.

Bergmann, Barbara (1987), ' "Measurement" or finding things out in economics', *Journal of Economic Education*, pp. 193–4.

Bergmann, Barbara and William Krause (1992), 'Evaluating and forecasting progress in the racial integration of employment', *Industrial and Labor Relations Review*, pp. 399–409.

Bergmann, Barbara (1994a), interview, 6 September 1994.

Bergmann, Barbara (1994b), 'Child care: the key to ending child poverty', Princeton Conference Paper on Social Policies for Children', May 25–27.

Bergmann, Barbara (1996a), *In Defense of Affirmative Action*, New York: Harper Collins, Basic Books.

Bergmann, Barbara (1996b), *Saving Our Children From Poverty: What the United States Can Learn From France*, New York: Russell Sage Foundation.

Hartmann, Heidi (1997), 'The economic emergence of women: Bergmann's six commitments', Meetings of the Allied Social Sciences Associations, New Orleans, 5 January.

McEachem, William (ed.) (1994), *The Teaching Economist*, Issue 8.

Ruskin, John (1891), 'Time and tide', *The Complete Works of John Ruskin*, vol. 14, Letter XIII, Philadelphia: Reuwee, Wattley & Walsh.

Index